D0938378

BBC

DOCTOR WHO

THE ELEVENTH DOCTOR

VOL 1: AFTER LIFE

"Amazing! It hit all the right notes, and got the Doctor perfect! 9/10"
COMIC BOOK CAST

"The characterization of the Doctor is spot on."
COMIC BOOK THERAPY

"10 out of 10!"
CULT DEN

"A fun read with some great characterization and a sense of adventure. 9 out of 10!"
COMICS VERSE

"An enjoyable romp."
FLICKERING MYTH

"9.5 out of 10!"
NERDS UNCHAINED

"Does a splendid job of capturing Matt Smith's expressions."
GEEK WITH CURVES

"The gorgeous artwork is used to tell the story in ingenious and touching ways."
HYPABLE

"A fantastic Eleventh Doctor adventure! 9 out of 10!"
NEWSARAMA

"A great job creating a companion who can keep up with the Doctor. 10 out of 10!"
PROJECT FANDOM

"Nails the tone and spirit right out of the gate. 4 out of 5!"
COMIC BOOK RESOURCES

"Superbly written. 9 out of 10!"
FLORIDA GEEK SCENE

"Captures the spirit of Matt Smith's version of the Eleventh Doctor!"
RETRENDERS

"A fun, quirky and emotional adventure."
UNLEASH THE FANBOY

"Compelling art."
BLEEDING COOL

"Well-written with great art!"
COMIC BASTARDS

TITAN COMICS

DOCTOR WHO: THE ELEVENTH DOCTOR VOL 1: AFTER LIFE
HB ISBN: 9781782761747 SB ISBN: 9781782763833

Published by Titan Comics, a division of
Titan Publishing Group, Ltd. 144 Southwark Street,
London, SE1 0UP.

A CIP catalogue record for this title is available from the British Library. First edition: April 2015.

10 9 8 7 6 5 4 3 2 1

Printed in China. TC0274.

Special thanks to
Steven Moffat, Brian Minchin, Matt Nicholls, Georgie Britton, Edward Russell, Derek Ritchie, Scott Handcock, Kate Bush, Julia Nocciolino, Ed Casey, Marcus Wilson and Richard Cookson for their invaluable assistance.

www.titan-comics.com

BBC

DOCTOR WHO

THE ELEVENTH DOCTOR

VOL 1: AFTER LIFE

WRITERS:
AL EWING & ROB WILLIAMS

ARTISTS:
SIMON FRASER
BOO COOK

COLORISTS:
GARY CALDWELL
HI-FI

LETTERS: RICHARD STARKINGS
AND COMICRAFT'S
JIMMY BETANCOURT

EDITOR:
ANDREW JAMES

DESIGNER:
ROB FARMER

THE DOCTOR

An alien who walks like a man. Last of the Time Lords of Gallifrey. Never cruel or cowardly, he champions the oppressed across time and space. Forever traveling, the Doctor lives to see the universe anew through the eyes of his human companions!

THE TARDIS

'Time and Relative Dimension in Space'. Bigger on the inside, this unassuming blue box is your ticket to unforgettable adventure!
The Doctor likes to think he's in control, but more often than not, the TARDIS takes him where and when he needs to be...

THE SONIC

An engineering marvel, the Sonic Screwdriver is a tool that scans, detects, unlocks and – yes! – unscrews. Vulnerable to deadlock seals and wood, it's still one of the Doctor's most treasured possessions. This year's model comes with claws and a green tip.

PREVIOUSLY...

After rebooting the universe with a second Big Bang, the Doctor has seen his new friends Amy and Rory married, and given them a honeymoon to remember.

Leaving the Ponds to settle into their newlywed life, the Doctor is traveling the cosmos alone, checking for anomalies in Reality 2.0 – a mission that is about to change his life forever!

When you've finished reading the collection, please email your thoughts to doctorwhocomic@titanemail.com

The sky was a cold, slate gray when Alice Obiefune buried her mother.
...AND THIS IS THE COMFORT OF THE GOOD.
THAT THE GRAVE CANNOT HOLD THEM, AND THAT THEY LIVE AS SOON AS THEY DIE. FOR DEATH IS NO MORE THAN A TURNING OF US OVER...
...FROM TIME INTO ETERNITY.
WILLIAM PENN.

Everything was gray.
Gray and barren and as cold as sharp stone.

After a few days, she returned to the library, working her usual shifts.
SEE, YOU PUT YOUR NAME IN THERE, IN THE LITTLE BOX -
Assisting the computer-illiterate, or just plain illiterate. Usually people the Department for Work and Pensions had turned away, since actually helping wasn't in their remit.

Once, thoughts like that had made her burn inside. Now she felt nothing.
"FOR THEY'VE BEEN TO THE LAKES, AND THE TORRIBLE ZONE, AND THE HILLS OF THE CHANKLEY BORE..."
02
And when she read to the children at storytime, she felt no joy.

She felt nothing but empty.
FRESCO
COOLI
Empty and gray.

Alice had looked after her mother for years; gradually, Ada Obiefune had become the cornerstone of her life.
Without that stone...
I'M SORRY, ALICE. WE DON'T WANT TO LOSE YOU, BUT...
CUTS.

...her life seemed to crumble.
...KNOCKING ALL THIS DOWN FOR FLATS. LUXURY FLATS, I MEAN. VERY HANDSOME OFFER.
NEED YOU OUT BY THE BEGINNING OF AUGUST, I'M AFRAID...

Everything just seemed to get worse. The grief. he grayness. The emptiness.
I KNOW WE'VE NOT TALKED IN A WHILE... I JUST FEEL LIKE MY WHOLE LIFE'S FALLING APART RIGHT NOW, AND YOU'RE THE ONLY FRIEND I'VE--
--YOU'RE MOVING TO WHERE?

Alice started to wonder if the grayness would ever end. If she'd ever feel anything but numb and empty again.
FRESCO
COOLI
Maybe she needed to see somebody.
EXCUSE ME!

Maybe she needed to see a--
EXCUSE ME!
COMING THROUGH!
81
FRES

CHAPTER 1

AFTER LIFE

WRITERS
AL EWING & ROB WILLIAMS

ARTIST
SIMON FRASER

COLORIST
GARY CALDWELL

LETTERER
RICHARD STARKINGS AND COMICRAFT'S JIMMY BETANCOURT

COOLI
ROWFF!

WELL, DON'T STAND THERE WITH YOUR FACE HANGING OUT!
...
RAINBOW DOG!

COME ON, WE'RE LOSING HIM!
I--
I WAS JUST--

COME ON!
And that's how it started.

HERE, BOY! HEEL! STAY!
TRY AND GRAB ITS TAIL--
NOT A TAIL!
EURR--
NOT THAT EITHER!
SORT OF A FEEDING-TUBE--ABSORBS ITS DIET FROM THE ATMOSPHERE AROUND IT!
AND THE FRONT END IS FOR...
OH, BARKING, LICKING, SNIFFING BOTTOMS - YOU KNOW, DOG STUFF!
ROWFF!
YEAH, BUT--BUT IT'S NOT A DOG, IS IT? IT'S SOME KIND OF--I DON'T KNOW, WEIRD ALIEN--
O!! NO NEED TO SAY IT LIKE THAT!
SOME OF US WEIRD ALIENS MIGHT TAKE OFFENSE!
...SORRY?
WELL, I SHOULD THINK SO TOO.
ALIENS ARE COOL.

I CAN'T--KEEP THIS UP MUCH LONGER...
NEARLY GOT HIM! GET READY TO GRAB THE TAIL!
YOU SAID IT WAS A--
SEMANTICS! GRAB THE TAIL!

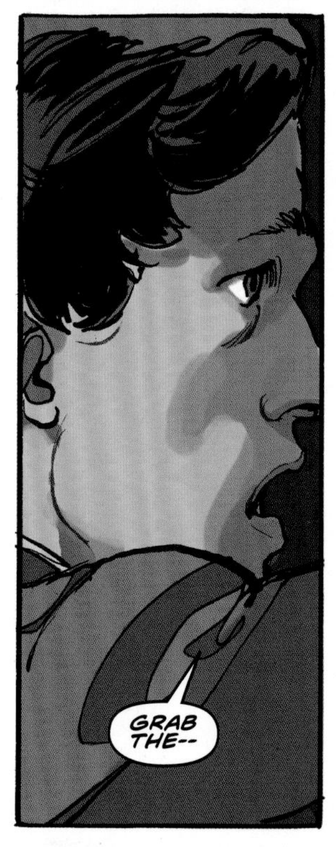
GRAB THE--

EXIT

...WHAT?

WHUNGGG

OW.
OH MY GOD! YOUR POOR NOSE!
NO, DON'T TILT YOUR HEAD BACK--HANG ON, I'LL GET A TISSUE--
And that's how it stopped.

He shook her hand.
Said he was very grateful for all her help and sorry it didn't work out.
I'B DER DOGDOR, BY DER WAY.
NICE DO BEET YOU.
FR

And before she could gather her thoughts and ask all the questions she would think of so many times afterwards... He walked around a corner and just...
...vanished.

Alice went back to her world. She had things to do, after all. A life to reclaim.
It was time to fight back.
HELLO? CITIZEN'S ADVICE?
LISTEN, I'M BEING EVICTED AND I THINK I MIGHT HAVE GROUNDS FOR--

It wasn't quite a happy ending...
...I'LL... I'LL... CALL YOU BACK.
VWOORRRP
VWOORRRP

...but the story wasn't over yet.
POLICE PUBLIC CALL BOX
VWOORRRP

HELLO! IT'S ME. THE DOCTOR. FROM EARLIER. WEIRD ALIEN NOSEBLEEDY LAMPPOST DOG MAN.
LISTEN, AH, I DON'T MEAN TO INTRUDE OR BE A BOTHER OR ANYTHING, IT'S JUST THAT... WELL...

YOU SEEMED SAD.

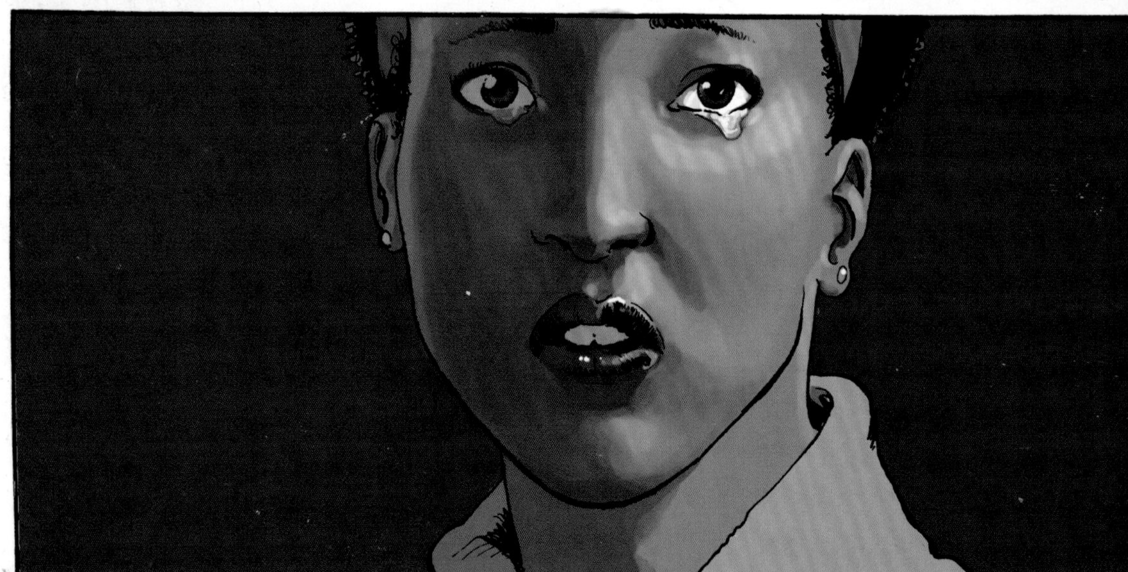

He made a cup of tea.
He didn't make silly remarks.
Or condescend. Or judge. Or pity. Or act like he was the important one in the room.
He just listened.

And after - after she'd got it all out, after she'd started to ask about him - he said:
POLIC
LISTEN... HOW DO YOU FEEL ABOUT HELPING ME CATCH A RAINBOW DOG?
BECAUSE I THINK THAT MIGHT BE FUN.

POLICI
I DON'T... SNFF I DON'T KNOW IF I CAN DO FUN... BUT...
BUT YOU HELPED ME CHASE A WEIRD ALIEN THROUGH THE STREETS OF LONDON THIS MORNING.
AND WHEN A VERY OUT OF SERVICE POLICE CALL BOX POPPED LITERALLY OUT OF NOWHERE IN YOUR FLAT, YOU DIDN'T RUN AWAY SCREAMING.

IT'S NOT ALWAYS FUN. T'S NOT ALWAYS SAFE. BUT IT IS ALWAYS...
...WELL.
WHY DON'T YOU OPEN THE DOOR AND SEE FOR YOURSELF?

...
GO ON, THEN.

IT...
IT'S...
YES, YES. GO ON AND SAY IT. THEY ALL SAY IT, YOU KNOW. NO SHAME IN IT. 'IT'S BIGGER ON THE...
IT'S ALL UPSIDE DOWN.
EH?
...WHATEVER IT IS.

WELL, WHAT ARE YOU WAITING FOR?
STEP IN. IT'S QUITE SAFE.
...ISH.

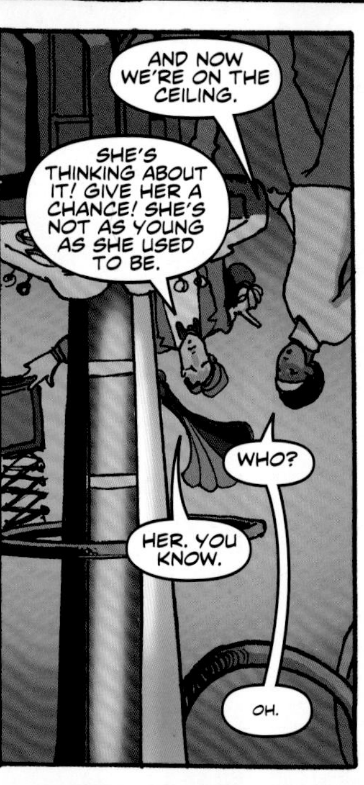
AND NOW WE'RE ON THE CEILING.
SHE'S THINKING ABOUT IT! GIVE HER A CHANCE! SHE'S NOT AS YOUNG AS SHE USED TO BE.
WHO?
HER. YOU KNOW.
OH.

WE'RE IN A DIFFERENT DIMENSION IN HERE, AREN'T WE?
YES! CLEVER!
I KNEW YOU WERE CLEVER, I CAN USUALLY TELL. WHAT DO YOU DO AGAIN?
I TOLD YOU I WAS A LIBRA ASSISTANT
BOOKS! THAT'LL BE IT. CLEVER AND BOOKS USUALLY GO TOGETHER.

SORRY. ≈SNFF≈ ROUGH WEEK. MONTH.

AH...
ERM..
...WELL SPOTTED!
GRAVITY STABILISERS HAVE BEEN PLAYING UP A BIT.
BEAR WITH ME!
...OKAY?

WHICH IS
HY I LOVE
RARIES! APART
OM THE ONES
HAT TRY AND
EAT ME.
WHAT IS ALL THIS?
TARDIS. IT'S A TIME MACHINE. OBVIOUSLY, LOOK AT ALL THE COOL STUFF.
A-HA! THE CULPRIT.
...ALICE?

SORRY. I'M SORRY. I THOUGHT I WAS... IT'S, IT'S JUST...
ALL THIS. ALL OF THIS HERE.
IT'S WONDERFUL. IT'S FROM SPACE.
AND I, AND I JUST LOOK AT IT ALL, AND... AND ALL I WANT...

I WANT HER TO SEE IT. THAT'S ALL. I WANT MUM TO BE HERE.
SHE'D LOVE IT.

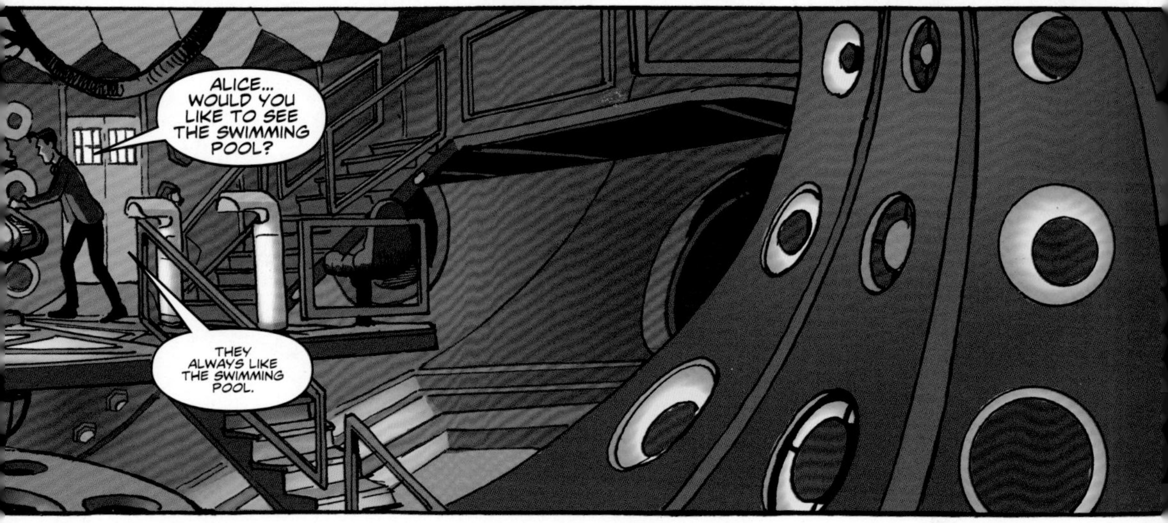
ALICE... WOULD YOU LIKE TO SEE THE SWIMMING POOL?
THEY ALWAYS LIKE THE SWIMMING POOL.

IT'S JUST YOU, THEN? NO FRIENDS? YOU TRAVEL ALONE?
SOMETIMES. RIGHT NOW? YES.
YES.

...WHEN I SHOWED YOU THE TARDIS. THE INSIDE.
HA! MY HEART WAS BEATING OUT OF MY CHEST.
YES, BUT YOU DIDN'T SHOW IT. DIDN'T DO THE OBVIOUS THING, DIDN'T SAY THE OBVIOUS THING. INSTEAD YOU DID SOMETHING I RATHER ADMIRE.

WHAT WAS THAT?
YOU SAW THAT SOMETHING WAS WRONG.
AND YOU POINTED IT OUT.

...YOU KEEP GOLDFISH IN HERE?
NOT **FISH**, MORE A HIGHLY INTELLIGENT AQUATIC RACE WHOSE WORLD WAS DESTROYED. I DON'T KEEP PETS. I MAKE **FRIENDS**.
THAT ONE'S CALLED REG, ACTUALLY.

FRIENDS.
LISTEN... WE'RE LOOKING FOR A WEIRD ALIEN, YEAH? BUT YOU CALL IT A DOG. IT DOES DOG STUFF. ESSENTIALLY, IT'S A DOG.
WELL... IT'S DOG-ISH. SORT OF.
COME ON.

TECHNICALLY? IT'S A KHARITITE. 'JOY-BEAST'. NATIVE TO THE PLANET VREULAR IN THE FIFTH GALAXY. I THINK THIS ONE FELL THROUGH A DIMENSIONAL RIFT.
IT HAD A TAG ON ITS EAR, DIDN'T IT? LIKE IT WAS MARKED. WHO'D DO THAT?
WELL... SCIENTISTS? YOU THINK IT ESCAPED FROM A LABORATORY?

OR...
OR? OR WHAT? DON'T DO CRYPTIC!
I DO CRYPTIC, I ALREADY BAGSIED CRYPTIC! YOU CAN'T HAVE CRYPTIC!
DOCTOR! WHO'D PUT A TAG ON A DOG?

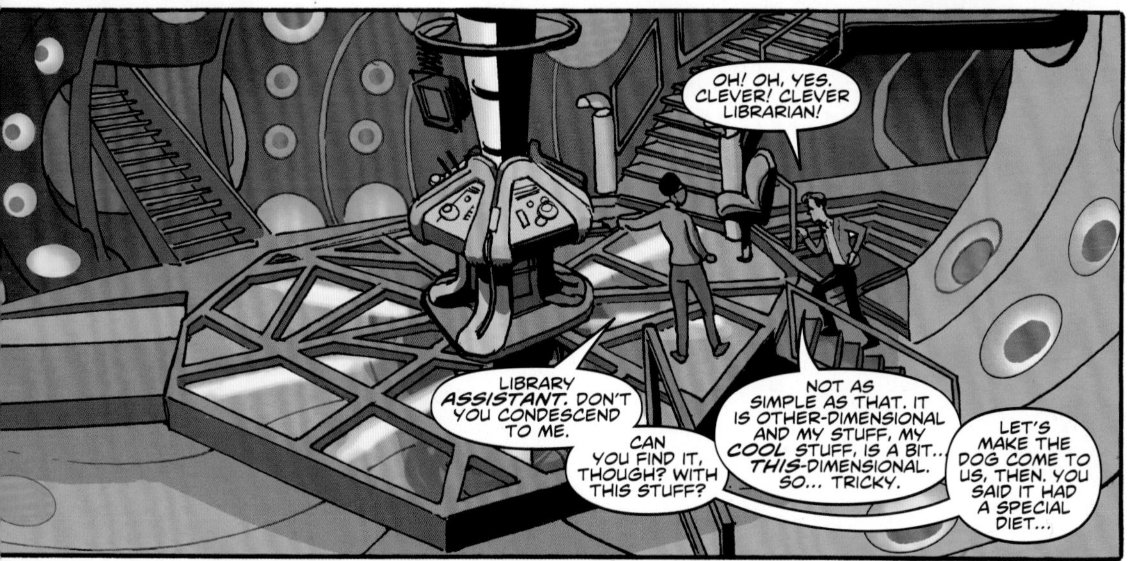
OH! OH, YES. CLEVER! CLEVER LIBRARIAN!
LIBRARY ASSISTANT. DON'T YOU CONDESCEND TO ME.
CAN YOU FIND IT, THOUGH? WITH THIS STUFF?
NOT AS SIMPLE AS THAT. IT IS OTHER-DIMENSIONAL AND MY STUFF, MY COOL STUFF, IS A BIT... THIS-DIMENSIONAL. SO... TRICKY.
LET'S MAKE THE DOG COME TO US, THEN. YOU SAID IT HAD A SPECIAL DIET...

KHARITITES ARE ATTRACTED TO SOMETHING SPECIFIC IN THE LOCAL ATMOSPHERE. THEY FEED ON IT. CONVERT IT INTO ENERGY AND MASS.
FEED ON WHAT?

MISERY. NEGATIVE EMOTIONS.
IT CAME BOUNDING UP TO YOU LIKE THAT BECAUSE YOU WERE SO UNHAPPY, ALICE. I'M SORRY.
AND... IT'S 2014. LOTS OF MISERY IN 2014. IT'LL EAT ITSELF TO DEATH IF WE DON'T FIND IT.
MIGHT EVEN TAKE A COUPLE OF TOP EMO BANDS WITH IT.

RIGHT. SO IT'S LOOKING FOR A LOT OF NEGATIVE EMOTIONS. IN LONDON.
AND IT'S, WHAT? MIDWEEK. LUNCHTIME?
I THINK I KNOW WHERE IT'S GOING.

HOUSE OF COMMONS, LONDON.
YERRRRRRR!
ORDER! ORDER!
HAHAHAHAHAHAH!

PRIME MINISTER'S QUESTIONS.
YERRRRRRR!
I SAY AGAIN! THE RIGHT HONORABLE GENTLEMAN WILL BE HEARD! I WOULD ASK BOTH SIDES OF THE HOUSE TO REMEMBER WHERE THEY ARE AND SHOW A GOOD EXAMPLE!
HERRRRRR

THANK YOU, MISTER SPEAKER.
AND I MUST SAY, IT'S PRETTY *RICH* FOR THE PARTY OPPOSITE TO BE SO VOCIFEROUS IN THEIR CONDEMNATION FOR A POLICY ENTIRELY NECESSARY BECAUSE OF THEIR FAILINGS.
AND IF I COULD SA *ONE* THING TO THE AND TO THE COUNTRY A WHOLE. IT WOULD THIS STATEMENT. POLITICAL *ETHOS* IF YOU WILL...
YERRRRRRR RRR!

BIG DOG! BIG DOG! REALLY BIG DOG!

AHHHHHH!!!
ORDER! ORDER!
MUMMY!!
YERRRRR!
OUT OF MY WAY! I'M IMPORTANT!

RASSHH
IT'S GETTING BIGGER.
IT'S GETTING A LOT BIGGER.
YES. HUMAN POLITICIANS AND A NEGATIVE EMOTIONS-GOBBLING KHARITITE? IT'S AN ALL YOU CAN EAT BUFFET.
HOW DO WE STOP IT GROWING?
GET EVERYONE TO LOVE EACH OTHER?

I DON'T THINK WE'VE GOT TIME--
STAY! STAY! THERE'S A GOOD KHARITITE EMPATHY BEAST!
KRASSSSHH
IT'S NO GOOD! I THINK HE STILL LIKES YOU!
LOOK OUT!!
YOU'RE-- HUFF--SOME SORT OF TIME TRAVELING ALIEN...
DON'T YOU HAVE SOME KIND OF HIGHLY ADVANCED SPACE GADGET TO--
RUN AWAAAY!
RIGHT! IT'S FOLLOWING YOU, ALICE. TRY AND DRAW IT OUTSIDE WHERE IT CAN'T HURT ANYONE, OR ITSELF.
WHAT? WHERE ARE YOU OFF TO?
SOMEWHERE ELSE. DON'T WORRY, I WILL COME BACK. PROBABLY.
ADMIT IT.
YOU'RE HAVING FUN, AREN'T YOU?

YEAH. THIS *IS* FUN.
THEY CAN PUT THAT ON MY GRAVESTONE.

ALICE UWAEBUKA OBIEFUNE. HAD FUN. THEN GOT CRUSHED TO DEATH BY GIANT ALIEN DOG--
--IN THE *HOUSE OF COMMONS*--

OH, HELLO, PRIME MINISTER.
I'VE BEEN WANTING A **WORD** WITH YOU.
BIG DOGGIE RUN RUN.
YEAH, MAYBE NOW'S NOT THE BEST...

KRASSSSSHHH
...TIME...

WHY'D IT GO OUTSIDE? IT'S NOT LIKE THERE'S ANY **MORE** NEGATIVE EMOTIONS--
OH NO.

ATTENTION UNSPECIFIED ALIEN ORGANISM!
YOU ARE ABOUT TO BE DISINTEGRATED BY THE UNIFIED INTELLIGENCE TASK FORCE!

MISTER PRIME MINISTER, SIR! PLEASE MOVE AS FAR AWAY FROM THE DISINTEGRATION AREA AS POSSIBLE!
NOW! THANK YOU!
YES... YES YES... EXCELLENT IDEA...

STOP! IT DOESN'T WANT TO HURT ANYONE!
STEP OUT OF THE WAY, MISS! OR YOU WILL BE DISINTEGRATED TOO!

NO!
THERE'S A SOLUTION HERE! THERE IS A SOLUTION HERE, AND IT'S NOT JUST--BLOWING THINGS UP!
WE CAN STILL MAKE THINGS BETTER!

VWOORRRP
VWOORRRP
VERY NICELY PUT.
TELEPHONE
FREE

...PRETTY BLUE BOX...

LICE PUBLIC CALL BO

AAAAAAHHH!

ANOTHER ALIEN! IT'S TAKEN OVER THE DOCTOR'S TARDIS!
OR 'E'S REGENERATED INTO SOMEFINK WELL 'ORRIBLE.
EITHER WAY! FIRE AT WILL--
WAIT!

IT'S NOT A THREAT!
THEN WHAT THE DEVIL IS IT, YOU FLOPPY BLIGHTER?
UNIT

...AND NOW A WALKING SQUID.
YES. YES, OF COURSE. OBVIOUSLY.

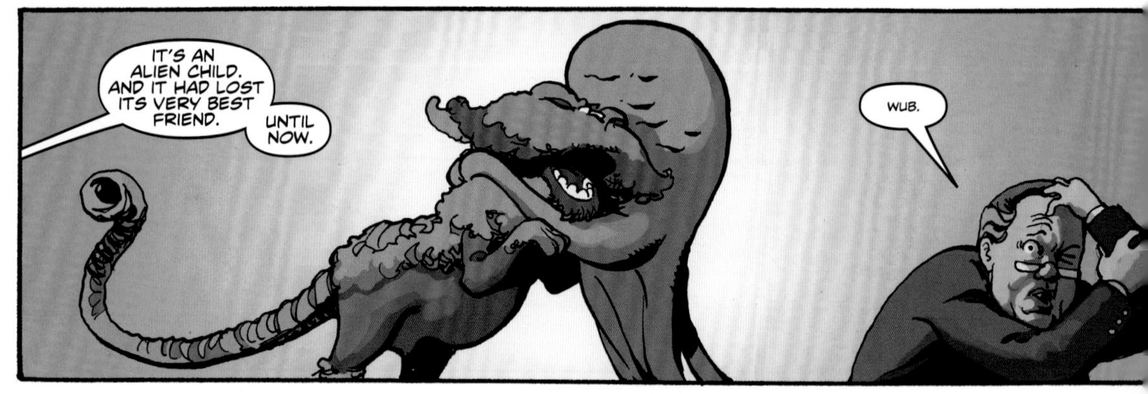
IT'S AN ALIEN CHILD. AND IT HAD LOST ITS VERY BEST FRIEND.
UNTIL NOW.
WUB.

DOCTOR, IT'S SHRINKING...
NO MORE SADNESS TO EAT. IT DIDN'T REALLY WANT OURS, ANYWAY. WE'RE NOT ITS SPECIAL FAVORITE.
IT ONLY EVER WANTED TO TAKE ONE BEING'S SADNESS AWAY.

POLICE BOX
COR. INNIT SWEET.
ISN'T IT? AND I WAS GUILTY OF THINKING OF IT AS ANOTHER... WEIRD ALIEN.
THE TARDIS TRACED THE KHARITITE'S SIGNAL BACK HOME. WHERE, IT TURNS OUT, IT WAS GREATLY MISSED.

YOU SEE, I DON'T KEEP PETS. I MAKE FRIENDS. BEST FRIENDS.
AND IT TOOK A VERY CLEVER FRIEND OF MINE TO REMIND ME THAT THEY'RE USUALLY THE SAME THING.

SHALL WE?
It wasn't quite a happy ending.

Lots of sadness left in the world.
SO THE SQUID SAID HELLO TO THE DOG. AND THEY WENT IN THE PRETTY BLUE BOX.
'COURSE THEY DID, SIR. UP YOU COME.
I WANT MY BEDDY NOW.

But somewhere, a child was playing with its best friend in all the universe...

And somewhere...
SO! ALICE OBIEFUNE. WHERE DO YOU WANT TO...
YOU COULD DROP ME OFF AT HOME. I'VE STILL GOT TO SORT OUT THE LANDLORD--

TIME FOR THAT LATER! ALL OF TIME AND SPACE, ANYWHERE AND ANYWHEN! YOU CAN DO BETTER THAN HOME!
I DON'T KNOW ABOUT THAT. BUT...
GO ON, THEN. LET'S GO SOMEWHERE...

...LET'S GO SOMEWHERE MUM WOULD HAVE LIKED.
POLICE BOX
...Somewhere...The story wasn't over yet.

And somewhere else...
...something waited.

CHAPTER 2

Cover C: Simon Fraser

DON'T YOU GIVE ME THAT LOOK!
I ASKED YOU A QUESTION!

LOOK, THIS IS MY FRIEND ALICE. SHE'S HAD A VERY HARD TIME OF IT LATELY --
DOCTOR, I'M NOT A PROP --
-- AND I REALLY WANTED TO TAKE HER SOMEWHERE NICE TODAY. FIRST TRIP IN THE TARDIS, SOMETHING TO REMEMBER.

I WANTED TO TAKE HER TO ROKHANDI.
THE MOST PERFECT PLANET IN THE UNIVERSE. JEWELLED MOUNTAINS, SINGING CANYONS, THE LESSER-SPOTTED CHROMATIC LIZARD. UNSPOILED NATURAL BEAUTY AS FAR AS THE EYE CAN SEE.
PRISTINE, PRESERVED AND PROTECTED BY A WHOLE SOLAR SYSTEM AS THEIR GREATEST LIVING TREASURE.

SO I LAND THE TARDIS ON ROKHANDI, I FLING THE DOOR OPEN AND LIKE A GREAT BERK I SHOUT "FEAST YOUR PEEPERS ON PARADISE!"
AND WHAT DO WE FEAST OUR PEEPERS ON? I'LL TELL YOU WHAT WE FEAST OUR PEEPERS ON!

WE FEAST OUR PEEPERS ON THIS!
DOES THIS LOOK UNSPOILED TO YOU?
... GAWRSH.
CUDDLES BEAR
MERRY
HEY
WOODY
JOY TOWN
Welcome to POKHANDI WORLD
a friendly World for All

WOULD YA LIKE A COMPLIMENTARY ROKHANDI FLOSS?
YES! NO! IT'S PROBABLY MADE OF HAIR!
DOCTOR --

GAWRSH, NO! IT'S FLASH-BOILED CHROMATIC LIZARD, FRESH FROM OUR BATTERY FARM!
TASTES LIKE CANDY!
GAHH!
DOCTOR! COME AWAY, FOR GOODNESS' SAKE --

YOU KNOW HE'S SPENT ALL DAY GETTING SHOUTED AT AND HARASSED ALREADY, RIGHT? THAT'S WHAT THEY HAVE TO PUT UP WITH AT THESE THEME PARKS.
SOME POOR GUY ON MINIMUM AGE, IN A BIG FOAM EAD IN THIS HEAT -- DOESN'T NEED YOU BANGING ON AT...
WAIT. HANG ON.

DID YOU JUST SAY WE WERE ON ANOTHER PLANET?
I'M BORED

I'M BORED
HELLO, SIR.

HOW WOULD YOU LIKE A FREE ROKHANDI FLOSS?

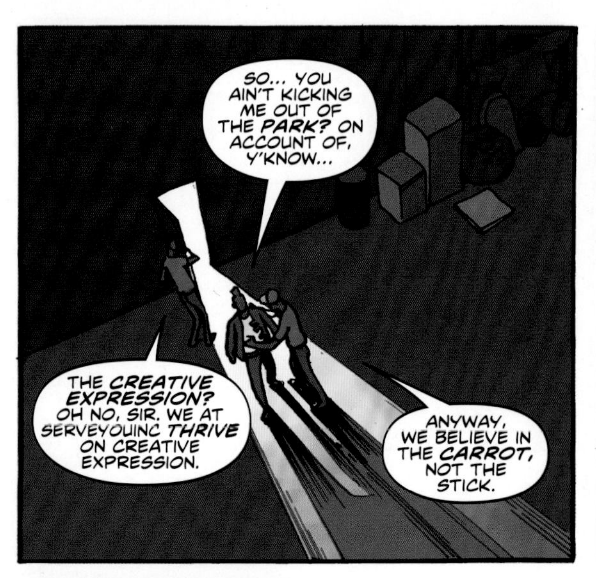
SO... YOU AIN'T KICKING ME OUT OF THE PARK? ON ACCOUNT OF, Y'KNOW...
THE CREATIVE EXPRESSION? OH NO, SIR. WE AT SERVEYOUINC THRIVE ON CREATIVE EXPRESSION.
ANYWAY, WE BELIEVE IN THE CARROT, NOT THE STICK.

THIS IS A FRIENDLY WORLD --
YEAH? WELL I AIN'T YOUR FRIEND, DWEEBO!
SURE YOU ARE.

WE'RE ALL FRIENDS HERE.
IT'S A FRIENDLY WORLD, A FRIENDLY WORLD, A FRIENDLY, FRIENDLY, FRIENDLY WORLD...
ANYWAY, WE'VE GOT YOUR FREE FLOSS RIGHT HERE.
HUH? WHERE? ALL I SEE IS THAT WEIRD KINDA --

SCHLUCK
A FRIENDLY WORLD, A FRIENDLY WORLD, A SUCH-GOOD-FRIENDS-TO-THE-END-LY WORLD...
ROKHANDI-WORLD IS A FRIENDLY WORLD...

SCHHLUUUURRRRF
...A FRIENDLY WORLD FOR AAAAALL...

CHAPTER 2

THE FRIENDLY PLACE

WRITER
AL EWING

ARTIST
SIMON FRASER

COLORIST
GARY CALDWELL

LETTERER
RICHARD STARKINGS AND COMICRAFT'S JIMMY BETANCOURT

PLASTIC.
EVERYTHING'S PLASTIC.

ARE YOU STILL SULKING?
LOOK, I WON YOU A STUFFED PIG ON THE SHOOTING GALLERY. HAVE A GOOD SHOUT AT IT, YOU'LL FEEL BETTER.

SHAN'T.
AND I'M NOT SULKING, IT JUST LOOKS LIKE I'M SULKING. IT'S SPECIAL TIME LORD... MEDITATIONAL... THINKY STUFF.
DOCTOR...

FINE! THERE'S A BIT OF SULKING MIXED IN. I CAN MULTI-TASK.
LOOK -- I'M ENJOYING MYSELF. I MEAN, A THEME PARK IN SPACE? IN THE FUTURE? THAT'S GREAT. MUM WOULD HAVE LOVED IT.
BUT... IF YOU'RE TRYING TO TELL ME ALL THIS SHOULDN'T BE HERE...

...LIKE IT'S SOME KIND OF, I DON'T KNOW, TEMPORAL ANOMALY --
OH, NO. IF IT WAS THAT, WE COULD RUN ABOUT AND TRY TO FIX IT. THERE'D BE MONSTERS AND BADDIES AND HAPPY ENDINGS. PROBABLY A MORAL.
IT'D BE FUN.
BUT THIS...

...THIS IS JUST HISTORY.
THAT'S WHAT'S SO SAD.

THIS PLANET. IT REALLY WAS... INDESCRIBABLE.
I MEAN, I COULD TALK YOUR EAR OFF ABOUT THE DIAMOND HUMMINGBIRDS AND THE FORESTS OF LIGHT AND, ALL RIGHT, THE CANDY-FLAVORED LIZARDS, BUT...
...WELL. IT'S JUST WORDS, ISN'T IT? JUST A LOAD OF SYLLABLES. IT'S NOT SEEING IT. FEELING IT.
I HAD TO SAVE THIS WHOLE SYSTEM FROM THE AMSTRONS OF THE GREAT WHEEL BEFORE THEY LET ME HAVE A PERMIT TO LAND HERE. TWICE.
THAT'S HOW PRECIOUS ALL THIS WAS. THAT'S WHAT I WANTED TO SHOW YOU, JUST HOW BEAUTIFUL THE UNIVERSE COULD BE. EXCEPT...
...EXCEPT I LANDED THE TARDIS WRONG. OVERSHOT. ONLY ABOUT... OH, TWENTY, THIRTY YEARS. MAYBE AS FEW AS TEN.
AN EYEBLINK.
THAT'S ALL HISTORY NEEDS.

THERE WAS A SHIFT IN GOVERNMENT.
AND THE NEW RULERS OF THE SYSTEM DECIDED THAT MAINTAINING ROKHANDI WAS AN... UNNECESSARY EXPENSE.
AND LET'S FACE IT, THEY WERE RIGHT. I MEAN, WHAT DOES A HUMMINGBIRD PROVIDE, EH?
WHAT DO CANDY LIZAR MANUFACTU WHAT PROFI THERE IN A CA THAT SINGS
SO THEY SOLD IT ALL.
THE FRIENDS OF THE RULERS GOT FIRST PICK, OF COURSE. LOVELY BIG BONUSES ALL ROUND. THERE WERE A FEW PETITIONS, BUT THERE ALWAYS ARE, AREN'T THERE?
AND WHO DOESN'T LOVE A THEME PARK?
GOOD THING I LANDED US HERE INSTEAD OF THE TOXIC WASTE MINES, REALLY.

SO... THERE WAS SOMETHING YOU LOVED VERY MUCH, AND IT... WENT *AWAY.* NOTHING YOU COULD DO ABOUT IT.
AND YOU JUST WANT TO *SCREAM* AND *CRY* AND TAKE IT *OUT* ON PEOPLE, EVEN THOUGH YOU KNOW THAT WON'T *CHANGE* ANYTHING.
THAT SOUND ABOUT RIGHT?
...YES.
SORRY.

BUT I AM *ALSO* DOING SPECIAL TIME LORD MEDITATIONAL THINKY STUFF. *REALLY!*
REALLY?
REALLY REALLY! I CAN MULTI-TASK. HERE, HAVE A LOOK AROUND YOU.

WHAT DO YOU *SEE?*

RIDES. STAFF. CUSTOMERS. HAPPY PEOPLE. WHAT AM I *LOOKING* FOR?
YOU NEARLY HAD IT. LET'S TURN THE QUESTION *AROUND* A LITTLE -- WHAT *DON'T* YOU SEE?

...
*UN*HAPPY PEOPLE.

YES! CLEVER LIBRARIAN!
LIBRARY ASSISTANT!
AND STOP SAYING IT LIKE I'M A DOG THAT GETS A TREAT!

HONESTLY, HAS ANYONE EVER TRIED TO THROTTLE YOU WITH THAT BOWTIE?
WELL, THIS ONE HAPPENS TO BE A CLIP-ON.
AND ALSO... YES. HENCE THE CLIP-ON.

ANYWAY, YOU SAID IT YOURSELF.
MINIMUM WAGE, HORRIBLE UNIFORMS, HOT SUN, PROBABLY SOME SORT OF ONGOING VOMIT SITUATION AROUND THE MORE ROLLER-Y COASTERS...
THEME PARK STAFF SHOULDN'T LOOK THIS... HAPPY.
ISN'T IT THEIR JOB, THOUGH? SMILE THROUGH THE PAIN AND THAT?

WELL, THAT'S JUST IT. EVEN THE MOST FERVENT BELIEVER IN THE JOYS OF CUSTOMER SERVICE STILL FEELS THE PAIN OF CLEANING UP A VOMIT-COASTER.
SMILES CRACK. OR ARE FAKED. BUT NOT HERE.

NOT JUST THE STAFF, EITHER. ALL THESE KIDS AND I HAVEN'T SEEN A SINGLE TANTRUM SINCE WE ARRIVED.
NO DRUNKS. NO PUSHING-IN IN THE QUEUES. POLITE, FRIENDLY CUSTOMERS, VOMITING QUIETLY IN THE BAGS PROVIDED.
ALMOST NO BAD BEHAVIOR AT...

...LET'S TRY AN EXPERIMENT.
WHERE'D YOU SAY YOU GOT THIS?

SPAK

UM... SIR, YOU'RE -- YOU'RE NOT SUPPOSED TO SHOOT CUSTOMER SERVICE PIG© --
SPAK
DON'T BE SILLY. HOW ELSE AM I SUPPOSED TO WIN ONE OF THESE PAPER TARGETS?
TARGE
HAPPY

I ALWAYS WANTED A PAPER TARGET. THEY BRIGHTEN UP THE HOME.
SPAK
OH DEAR, S HEAD CAME F. THIS GAME'S BIT VIOLENT, 'T IT? MIND YOU, CHILDREN LIKE THAT.
SIR, PLEASE, YOU'RE DOING IT WRONG -- YOU'RE MEANT TO SHOOT THE TARGETS TO WIN THE TOYS --

A PAPER TARGET IS AN EXCELLENT TOY. YOU CAN PIN IT UP AND THROW STONES AT IT. PRETEND YOU'RE IN AN EXCITING... STONE BATTLE.
NO BATTERIES REQUIRED, JUST A BIT OF CREATIVE EXPRESSION --
AND WE THRIVE ON CREATIVE EXPRESSION.

HELLO, SIR.
WOULD YOU LIKE A COMPLIMENTARY ROKHANDI FLOSS?

INTERESTING. EVERY TIME I ACT UP, YOU LOT OFFER ME SWEETS. BUYING ME OFF?
WE BELIEVE IN THE CARROT, SIR. NOT THE STICK.
HOW ABOUT A FREE ROKHANDI-WORLD T-SHIRT?

ONE HUNDRED PER CENT COTTON. ALL YOUR FAVORITE MASCOTS -- CUSTOMER SERVICE PIG©, TEAM-BUILDING EXPERIENCE HORSE©...
OOOH! NO. WHAT ELSE HAVE YOU GOT?
WHATEVER MAKES YOU HAPPY, SIR. COMPLIMENTARY HOTEL ROOM? FREE BREAKFAST?

PAPER TARGET?
EVERYBODY WANTS SOMETHING, SIR.

...ANSWERS TO QUESTIONS.
WELL, I DON'T HAVE MANY OF THOSE, SIR. I'M A VERY RECENT HIRE BY THE COMPANY.

COMPANY?
SERVEYOUINC, SIR. WE'RE ALL FRIENDS HERE.
COME WITH ME...

OH, HELLO AGAIN, MISS! WHAT ARE YOU STILL DOING HERE?
I'M WONDERING THE SAME THING.
THAT HAPPEN A LOT, THEN?

PEOPLE MAKE TROUBLE AND THEN GET LED OFF SOMEWHERE?
WELL, GEE.
WHEN YOU SAY IT LIKE THAT, IT SOUNDS SINISTER.

MOSTLY IT'S FOLKS WHO JUST LANDED, THOUGH -- THE ONES WHO DON'T GET HOW FRIENDLY THINGS ARE HERE.
BUT IT'S OKAY. THE SECURITY STAFF HAVE A TALK WITH THEM AND THEY'RE JUST GOOD AS GOLD AFTER THAT. GOOD AS GOLD.
HECK, SOME OF THEM EVEN START WORKING HERE. I MEAN, I DID.

SEE, BEFORE I CAME FOR A VACATION HERE, I WAS JUST BUMMING AROUND, NOT DOING MY BIT -- NO USE TO ANYONE, RIGHT? BUT THEN --
YEAH, GOTTA GO. I'VE GOT A...
SIGH
...I'VE GOT A FRIEND TO CATCH UP WITH.

UH...
I NEED THE GUN BACK?

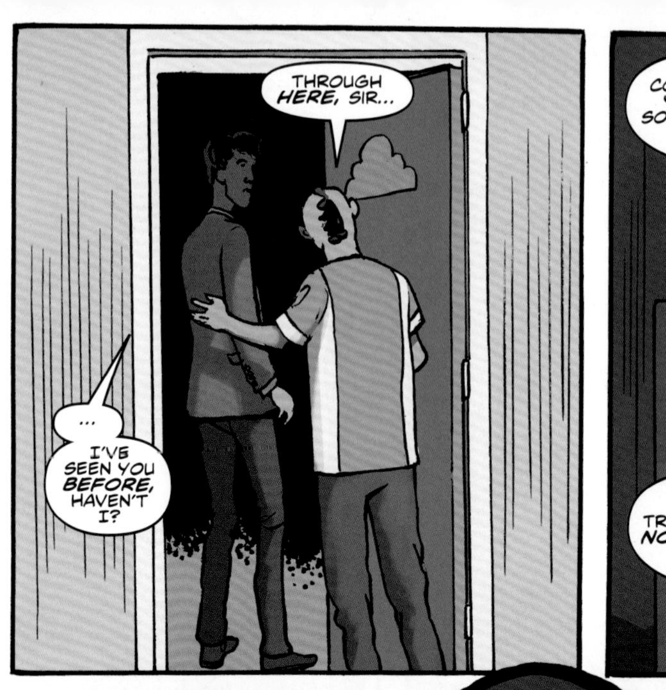
THROUGH HERE, SIR...
... I'VE SEEN YOU BEFORE, HAVEN'T I?

OUT OF THE CORNER OF MY EYE. YOU WERE DOING SOMETHING NAUGHTY WITH A SPRAY CAN.
MISBEHAVING.
VERY LIKELY, SIR. I WAS A TROUBLED YOUTH. BUT NOW... I'VE LEARNED HOW TO MAKE FRIENDS.
IT'S A FRIENDLY WORLD, A FRIENDLY WORLD, ROKHANDI-WORLD IS A FRIENDLY WORLD...

...A FRIENDLY WORLD FOR ALL.
HELLO, SIR.
WE'VE GOT YOUR FREE FLOSS RIGHT HERE.

HE DIDN'T WANT THE FLOSS, BOSS.
YOUR T-SHIRT, THEN. ONE HUNDRED PER CENT COTTON. JUST STEP A LITTLE CLOSER...
YES, ACTUALLY IF YOU DON'T MIND I THINK I'LL STAY OVER HERE...

IT'S OKAY. IT DOESN'T HURT OR NYTHING. AND YOU'LL FEEL SO MUCH ORE FRIENDLY AFTERWARDS, YOU WON'T MAKE TROUBLE AT ALL.
WE MIGHT EVEN GIVE YOU A JOB.
A JOB WITH A FUTURE.

TOXIC WASTE MINING IS A JOB WITH A FUTURE.
QUITE A SHORT ONE, I'M GUESSING.
AND WHILE I'M GUESSING, LET'S JUST SEE IF I'VE GOT THIS RIGHT...

WHATEVER THIS... THIS ENTITY IS, IT'S SOME SORT OF MENTAL PARASITE. IT FEEDS OFF WILL, AMBITION, CREATIVITY, THE DESIRE TO... WELL, MAKE TROUBLE. IT'S ALL TIED TOGETHER.
SO PEOPLE COME ERE TO ESCAPE FROM THE HARSH REALITIES OF HE MODERN ERA, AND THE PROBLEM ELEMENTS AMONG THEM LEAVE... PACIFIED.
MORE ABLE TO ACCEPT THEIR LOT.

SURE. SOME OF US. SOME OF US DON'T LEAVE AT ALL.
WHY WOULD WE?
ROKHANDI-WORLD IS A FRIENDLY WORLD. A FRIENDLY WORLD FOR --

SPAK
OWW!

LET GO OF HIM!
NEXT ONE TO MOVE GETS IT IN THE FRONT END! I MEAN IT!

ALICE OBIEFUNE, GUN-TOTING LIBRARIAN! BRILLIANT!
THOUGH GENERALLY SPEAKING, SHOOTING PEOPLE IN THE BOTTOM WITH GUNS IS NOT OKAY ON THESE TRIPS. MENTAL NOTE FOR LATER.
DOCTOR, HURRY UP! WE NEED TO --
AHEM.
-- ESCAPE.
AH.

AND YOU WOULD BE...
AUGUST HART, DOCTOR. YOU REMEMBER.
THEY DEMOTED ME, YOU KNOW. MADE ME CHIEF SECURITY OFFICER OF THIS... RIDICULOUS LITTLE SIDESHOW.

SO WHEN I SAW YOUR FACE ON THE SECURITY CAMERAS... MAKING TROUBLE, AS USUAL... WELL. I HAD TO SEE TO YOU PERSONALLY.
AND MISS OBIEFUNE AS WELL! HOW DELIGHTFUL! YOU CAN BE PROCESSED TOGETHER.
...SORRY, DO I KNOW YOU?

NOW, WHERE'S THE OTHER ONE?
WHAT OTHER ONE? DOCTOR, WHO IS THIS?
...NO IDEA.

BUT I KNOW THE TYPE. MR... HART, WAS IT?
CHIEF SECURITY OFFICER HART!
YES, I KNOW YOU, MR HART. I KNOW JUST WHAT YOU ARE. YOU'RE A CLASSIC BULLY WITH A BIT OF SADIST THROWN IN, AREN'T YOU?

HOW DARE YOU --
THOUGHT SO. YOU'RE JUST NOT A CARROT PERSON, MR HART. YOU'RE STICK, STICK, STICK ALL THE WAY.
SO... WHY THIS APPROACH?

WHY NOT JUST HIT BANKSY JUNIOR HERE OVER THE HEAD AND BUNDLE HIM INTO THE BEAST'S LAIR? NOBODY WOULD CARE. OR EVEN NOTICE.
WHY DOES IT MATTER WHA TROUBLEMAKER WANT?
...BECAUSE IT'S PART OF THE FEEDING PROCESS?

LIKE THIS THING NEEDS YOU TO KIND OF... INVITE IT INTO YOUR MIND. IT GIVES YOU WHAT YOU WANT, SO YOU OPEN YOURSELF UP TO IT.
VERY GOOD! CLEVER, CLEVER LIBR --
DOCTOR? I'VE GOT A GUN. AND YOU'VE GOT A BUM.

...CLEVER... LIBRARY ASSISTANT?
YES, WELL DONE, MISS OBIEFUNE. YOU'RE QUITE RIGHT, OF COURSE. THE ENTITY IS A SIMPLE CREATURE, BUT REMARKABLY EFFECTIVE AT BREAKING INTO CLOSED MINDS.
IT SHARES A PERFECT MENTAL IMAGE WITH YOU OF WHAT YOU WANT. WHAT YOU CAN'T RESIST.

SMALL, PETTY THINGS, USUALLY. T-SHIRTS. COMPLIMENTARY BREAKFASTS. PEOPLE SIGN AWAY THEIR SOULS FOR SO LITTLE...
AND THEN IT TAKES ALL THOSE... DIFFICULT PARTS OF YOU... AND DIGESTS THEM. SLOWLY.
OBVIOUSLY, IT HELPS THE PROCESS IF THE SUBJECT APPROACHES VOLUNTARILY. HENCE THE CARROT.

BUT THE CARROT IS FAR FROM ESSENTIAL.
GRAB THEM.

DOCTOR -- AAOW!
ALICE!
DRAG THEM INTO RANGE. IT'LL BE OVER SOON, DOCTOR.
SOON... YOU'LL BE GOOD AS GOLD.

NO -- WAIT, YES! DRAG US INTO RANGE!
YOU! MISTER CHEWING GUM! THERE'S SOMETHING I WANT!
COME AND GET --

-- IT --
SCHLUCCK

DOCTOR! NO!
RRRR --
SCHLUUUUU-

--HORRRP!

WHAT -- WHAT WAS I -- WAIT, YOU FED ME TO THAT THING?
I -- I DIDN'T KNOW WHAT I WAS DOING -- THEY MADE ME --
SECURITY!

I NEED EXTRACTION OFF-WORLD -- THE ENTITY'S BEEN DESTABILISED, AND THEY'RE -- THEY'RE ALL REMEMBERING --
WE'RE ALL REMEMBERING, YOU SCUMBAG! YOU'RE GOING NOWHERE! AND WHEN WE FIND YOU --
DOCTOR!
I'LL KILL YOU FOR THIS!

YOU'VE MADE AN ENEMY THERE. WHAT HAPPENED, DOCTOR?
WELL, IT'S LIKE HART SAID. THE ENTITY IS A SIMPLE CREATURE. AND MOST PEOPLE ONLY WANT SMALL THINGS -- T-SHIRTS, GALACTIC EMPIRES, ETERNAL LIFE.
I DECIDED I WANTED SOMETHING BIG.

AN ARRAY OF TWO HUNDRED AND EIGHT DIFFERENT FORTY-THREE-DIMENSIONAL SUPERSOLIDS. ALL SUPERIMPOSED.
PART OF MY HIGHER-DIMENSIONAL PHYSICS DEGREE AT DEAR OLD TIME LORD UNIVERSITY. LEARNING TO ENVISION IT TOOK ME ROUGHLY EIGHT YEARS.
I THINK I MADE IT THROW UP.

WELL, YOU CAN'T HAVE A THEME PARK WITHOUT VOMIT.
No Unauthorized Personnel
EXACTLY. AND LUCKILY, THE ENTITY DIGESTS SLOWLY ENOUGH THAT MOST PEOPLE WILL HAVE GOTTEN THEIR ORIGINAL MINDS BACK.
I'M GUESSING THERE ARE A LOT OF NAUGHTY THOUGHTS OUT IN ROKHANDI-WORLD...

WAAAAAHHH! I HATE YOU I HATE YOU I HATE YOU!
NOW THERE'S THE THEME PARK EXPERIENCE I REMEMBER.
OH, I AM SO BORED... I GOTTA QUIT THIS STINKIN' JOB AND GET THE BAND BACK TOGETHER...
GET THE HECK AWAY FROM ME, YA LITTLE VERMIN! I GOTTA GET OUT OF THIS HEAD! IT'S A HUNDRED DEGREES!

PLUS YOU GOT YOUR MONSTER AND YOUR BADDIE AND YOUR HAPPY ENDING. WELL, HAPPY-ISH.
HORRRP
YES, I CAN'T SEE SERVEYOUINC SURVIVING THIS LITTLE SCANDAL...

POLICE PUBLIC CALL BOX
AND WE EVEN GOT A MORAL.
OOH! I'VE GOT THIS! LET'S SEE, SOMETHING ABOUT CHANGE... EVEN PERFECT WORLDS HAVE TO END SOMETIME, BUT AS LONG AS THERE'S THE WILL TO --
NAH.

THE MORAL IS... NEXT TIME, WATCH WHEN YOU'RE LANDING.
VWOORRRP
...
CLEVER LIBRARIAN.
VWOORRRP

EPILOGUE:
...SO ROKHANDI IS A DISASTER AREA. THE PARK IS A DEAD LOSS, THE MINE WORKERS ARE STRIKING...
...AND THERE'S EVEN TALK OF A FULL-SCALE REVOLUTION AGAINST OUR FRIENDS IN SYSTEM GOVERNMENT.
ALL THANKS TO THE SAME MYSTERIOUS 'DOCTOR' WHO COST US THE ARC EXPERIMENT TEN YEARS AGO.
THERE HAD BEST BE SOME GOOD NEWS, PROFESSOR DUTTA.
N-NO, SIR. IN FACT... THERE MAY BE, UH... WORSE NEWS.
YOU SEE, WHEN WE LOST THE PORTION OF THE ENTITY THAT WAS ON ROKHANDI...

...IT DID SOMETHING TO THE REST OF IT...

CHAPTER 3

Cover C: Simon Fraser

OCKERY PLANTATION, MISSISSIPPI, 1931.
"STANDIN' AT THE CROSSROAD, BABY, RISIN' SUN GOIN' DOWN..."
"I BELIEVE TO MY SOUL, NOW, POOR BOB IS SINKIN' DOWN"...

WOOOOOOH!
YEAH!
THANK YOU. THAT'S KIND OF Y'ALL.

...OH MY...
TOUGH CROWD. EAT YOU ALIVE. YOU SCARED?
YESSIR.

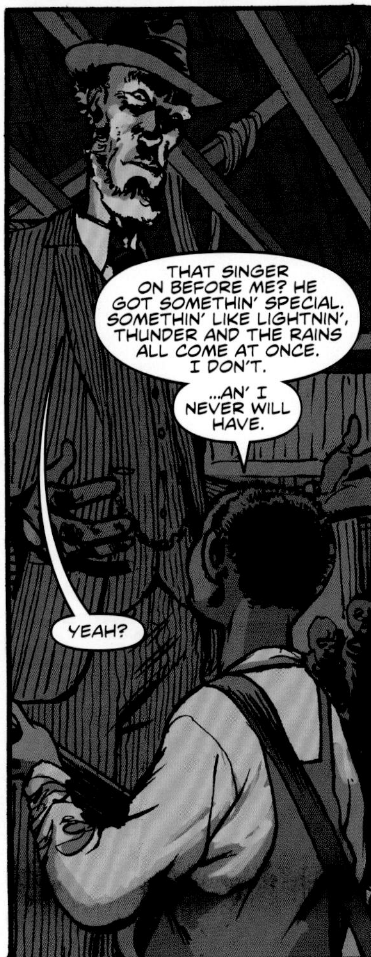
THAT SINGER ON BEFORE ME? HE GOT SOMETHIN' SPECIAL. SOMETHIN' LIKE LIGHTNIN', THUNDER AND THE RAINS ALL COME AT ONCE. I DON'T.
...AN' I NEVER WILL HAVE.
YEAH?

I'M THE TALENT SCOUT.
WHAT IF I TOLD YOU SIX DAYS AGO THAT BOY WAS WAY WORSE THAN YOU ON THEM HARD STRINGS.
THWIP

AND THEN I TOLD HIM 'BOUT SOMEONE HE COULD GO SEE. OUT THERE IN THE BAYOU. AT MIDNIGHT. SOMEONE WHO HE COULD MAKE A DEAL WITH...
SOMEONE WHO COULD GIVE HIM WHAT HE WANTS MOST... FOR A PRICE.
SERVEYOU INC

SO, GUESS THERE'S A QUESTION YOU NEED TO ASK YOURSELF...

HOW BAD YOU WANNA BE GOOD?

RUMMMBLE
RUMMMBLE
HELLO?

HELLO.
AAAAAHH!

STATE NATURE OF ABILITY YOU WISH TO BE UPGRADED.
AH! GUITAR! I WANT... I WANT TO ABLE TO PLAY... LIKE IN MY DREAMS!
ACKNOWLEDGED. DO YOU AGREE TO ALL SERVEYOUINC TERMS AND AGREEMENTS? VERBALIZE AFFIRMATIVE TO BEGIN IMPROVEMENT PROCESS.
FTHOOOOOOONNNN

YOU REALLY DON'T WANT TO BE SAYING YES TO THAT, MATE.
GO HOME AND PRACTICE, THAT'S MY ADVICE. GO ON NOW. IF YOU WANT TO LIVE! RUN...
GO ON!! PEG IT!!!
STATE NATURE OF ABILITY...
PHWWWWWTTTT
AAAAAAHHH!!
JONES! I HAVE NO IDEA HOW TO DRIVE THIS THING, SO GET THE DOCTOR IN, QUICK!
WHO 1
ROAAAAAARRRRRRR
GET HIM IN THE MONSTER TRUCK!
THEY GAVE THE DOCTOR WHAT HE WANTS!

CHAPTER 3

WHAT HE WANTS...

WRITER
ROB WILLIAMS

ARTIST
SIMON FRASER

COLORIST
GARY CALDWELL

LETTERER
RICHARD STARKINGS AND COMICRAFT'S JIMMY BETANCOURT

LONDON, 2014.
EARLIER...
SUPPOSE I SHOULD TRY AND SELL THEM. THEY MIGHT BE WORTH SOMETHING.

CAN'T BELIEVE MUM KEPT ALL THESE RUBBISH OLD ALBUMS.
IF YOUR MUM LOVED THEM, THEY ARE WORTH SOMETHING, ALICE. UNLESS THEY'RE POLKA DANCES. IN WHICH CASE, IGNORE MY LAST STATEMENT.
POLICE PUBLIC CALL BO
HMM... MIGHT NEED TO BREATHE IN A BIT TO GET HER THROUGH...

AH, THIS IS MORE LIKE IT. DELTA BLUES. JAZZ. SHE WAS CRAZY ABOUT ALL THAT OLD STUFF.
ROBERT JOHNSON
KING OF THE DELTA BLUES
LOVED HER SOME REGGAE TOO.

WHO DOESN'T? "IRIE, MON!" AS I ONCE REPROGRAMMED A CYBERMAN TO SAY. REPEATEDLY.
POLICE
AW... LOOK AT THIS. DEFINITELY NOT RUBBISH!

NOW THIS WAS HER FAVOURITE.
ABANAZAR'S MADNESS
WELL, ALL OF HIS WERE. THE ULTIMATE POP STAR, SHE USED TO TELL ME. SHE SAW HIM LOADS OF TIMES.
HE PLAYED HIS EARLY SHOWS AROUND HERE, YOU KNOW. JUST A COUPLE OF STREETS AWAY, IN A CLUB THEY KNOCKED DOWN.

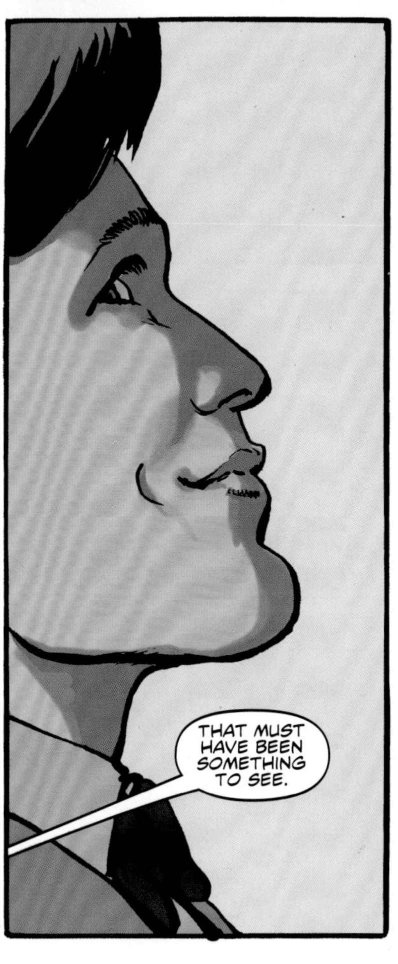
THAT MUST HAVE BEEN SOMETHING TO SEE.

1962.
A COUPLE OF STREETS AWAY...
DOG & DUCK
TONIGHT
JOHN JONES
POP
LITTER
ADAMS
YOU ARE HAVING A LAUGH!
FIRST, BEST USE OF A TIME MACHINE, ALICE -- GOING TO SEE ALL THE CLASSIC GIGS IN THE UNIVERSE THAT YOU'VE ONLY EVER READ ABOUT.

CASE IN POINT: YOU KNOW THE BEATLES' FIRST SHOW AT THE CAVERN CLUB, 1961?
YES.
96% OF THE AUDIENCE WERE TIME TRAVELLERS. ACTUALLY, SO WAS LENNON, BUT THAT'S A DIFFERENT STORY.

YEAH, BUT... THIS? THIS IS JOHN JONES' FIRST EVER SHOW?
THE CHAMELEON OF POP? THE TALL PALE EARL? XAV MOONBURST HIMSELF?

HE WAS SUCH A BEAUTIFUL FREAK, MUM ALWAYS SAID IT WAS LIKE HE'D COME FROM ANOTHER PLANET.

WELL, YES. SPEAKING ON BEHALF OF BEAUTIFUL FREAKS FROM OTHER PLANETS...
PLEASE GIVE A BIG DOG & DUCK WELCOME TO... JOHN JONES!
TICKETS
OHMYGOD, SHUSH! HE'S ON! GET READY, DOCTOR! GET READY FOR THE COSMIC POP EXPLOSION. HERE IT COMES...

UM.... 'ELLO.
THIS ON? ANYONE HEAR ME? I DON'T THINK THIS IS ON.
EXIT
TAP TAP

NIGEL. NIGEL. I'M FAIRLY CONFIDENT THIS ISN'T ON.
IT'S ON, JOHN.
NO, NIGEL, WERE I A BETTING MAN, I'D CONFIDENTLY WAGER THAT THIS ISN'T ON.
IT'S DEFINITELY ON, JOHN.

OH NO.
AH.
HE HAS LESS STAGE PRESENCE THAN ANY HUMAN BEING THAT'S EVER LIVED.
SO IT WOULD APPEAR...
NO, NIGEL, I REMAIN FIRMLY CONVINCED THAT THE MICROPHONE IS NOT CURRENTLY OPERATIONAL.

IT DOESN'T MAKE SENSE. NOT ONE PERSON IN THAT CLUB EVEN NOTICED HE WAS ONSTAGE. AND HIS SONGS? WHAT WAS THAT PIXIE THING?
PEOPLE... ROGRESS?
NOT *THAT* MUCH! HE BECOMES THE MOST CHARISMATIC POP SINGER IN HISTORY! HOW ON EARTH DOES HE BECOME THE MOST CHARISMATIC POP SINGER IN HISTORY?

PERHAPS HE EATS HIS GREENS? DOES LOTS OF SIT-UPS?
UNBELIEVABLE... ALL MY LIFE, MUM TOLD ME HOW AMAZING THAT JOHN JONES SHOW WAS, AND WHAT ACTUALLY HAPPENED...? *IT WAS RUBBISH!*

JOHN JONES, IT TURNS OUT, HAS NO TALENT WHATSOEVER!!
...OH.

NOW, NOW. IF I'VE LEARNT ONE THING OVER 900 YEARS, ALICE, IT'S THAT EVERYONE HAS TALENT. EVEN IF IT'S SOMETIMES... EXTREMELY WELL HIDDEN.
...BIT 'ARSH.
POP

DAVROS, FOR INSTANCE. ON FIRST GLANCE YOU DON'T GO: "NOW THERE'S SOMEONE WHO'S A WHIZZ AT REALITY BOMBS".
...NOT 'AVING IT.

WHO'S DAVROS? GREEK BLOKE?
ERM... NOT EXACTLY.
AH, I'M SORRY. IT'S JUST. THAT WAS LIKE... IT INSULTED MUM, IN A WAY. I THOUGHT I KNEW HER, Y'KNOW? BUT IF SHE'S WRONG ABOUT THIS...

I THOUGHT I WAS GOING TO SEE ONE OF HISTORY'S ALL-TIME GREAT ARTISTS.

ALICE OBIEFUNE, HISTORY IS FULL OF ALL-TIME GREAT ARTISTS.
YOU'RE CURRENTLY LUCKY ENOUGH TO BE STANDING IN THE PRESENCE OF ONE, IN FACT.

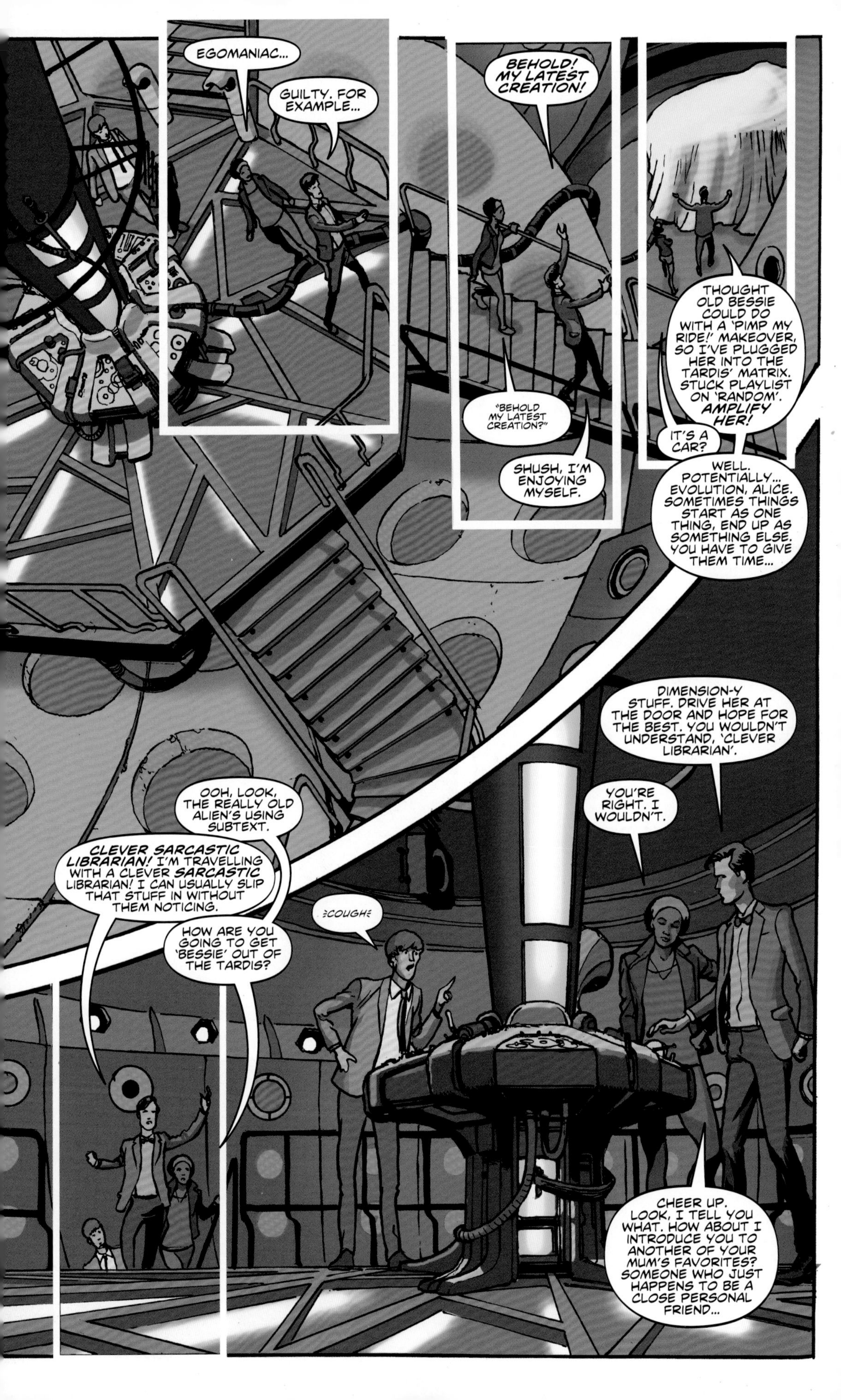
EGOMANIAC...
GUILTY. FOR EXAMPLE...
BEHOLD! MY LATEST CREATION!
"BEHOLD MY LATEST CREATION?"
SHUSH, I'M ENJOYING MYSELF.
THOUGHT OLD BESSIE COULD DO WITH A 'PIMP MY RIDE!' MAKEOVER, SO I'VE PLUGGED HER INTO THE TARDIS' MATRIX. STUCK PLAYLIST ON 'RANDOM'. AMPLIFY HER!
IT'S A CAR?
WELL. POTENTIALLY... EVOLUTION, ALICE. SOMETIMES THINGS START AS ONE THING, END UP AS SOMETHING ELSE. YOU HAVE TO GIVE THEM TIME...
DIMENSION-Y STUFF. DRIVE HER AT THE DOOR AND HOPE FOR THE BEST. YOU WOULDN'T UNDERSTAND, 'CLEVER LIBRARIAN'.
YOU'RE RIGHT. I WOULDN'T.
OOH, LOOK, THE REALLY OLD ALIEN'S USING SUBTEXT.
CLEVER SARCASTIC LIBRARIAN! I'M TRAVELLING WITH A CLEVER SARCASTIC LIBRARIAN! I CAN USUALLY SLIP THAT STUFF IN WITHOUT THEM NOTICING.
COUGH
HOW ARE YOU GOING TO GET 'BESSIE' OUT OF THE TARDIS?
CHEER UP. LOOK, I TELL YOU WHAT. HOW ABOUT I INTRODUCE YOU TO ANOTHER OF YOUR MUM'S FAVORITES? SOMEONE WHO JUST HAPPENS TO BE A CLOSE PERSONAL FRIEND...

MISSISSIPPI, 1931.
VWOORRRP VWOORRRP
THUMMMMMM

DOCTOR, IT'S OKAY. I'M NOT A CHILD HAVING A TANTRUM. MUM WAS A HUMAN BEING. HUMAN BEINGS EXAGGERATE. MEMORIES SHIFT OVER THE YEARS.
I KNOW SHE WAS MORE THAN JUST MY MUM. SHE WAS A... PERSON. A WHOLE, REAL... PERSON.

AH...
ALICE OBIEFUNE.

I SO OFTEN TRAVEL WITH YOUNG PEOPLE. DO YOU KNOW... IT IS RATHER NICE TO SPEND TIME WITH SOMEONE CLOSER TO MY OWN AGE.
CHEEKY. I'M NOT THAT OLD.
I WAS THINKING MORE IN TERMS OF WISDOM. SOMEONE WITH A SENSE OF COOL, UNFLAPPABLE GRAVITAS THAT MATCHES MY OW...

OI! YOU TWO!
AH!
AHHHHHHH!!
POLICE PUBLIC CALL BO

I HEARD YOU TWO SLAGGING ME OFF OUTSIDE THE CLUB. YOU OUGHT TO BE ASHAMED OF YOURSELVES.
WHA... WHA... JOHN JONES, WHAT ARE YOU DOING HERE?
WRRRRRRR

FOLLOWED YOU, DIDN'T I? FROM OUTSIDE THE CLUB, WHERE I HEARD YOU BESMIRCHING MY AUDIOPHONIC TALENTS!
NOT POSSIBLE. THAT... THAT'S NOT POSSIBLE. I'M THE DOCTOR. I ALWAYS KNOW WHO'S ON THE TARDIS. MOSTLY.
WRRRRRRR

YOU! YOU FOLLOWED US INTO THE TARDIS AND I DIDN'T KNOW YOU WERE THERE! AND NOW YOU'VE TRAVELLED BACK IN TIME TO THE MISSISSIPPI DELTA, 1931.
THAT'S... REMARKABLE!
YOU'RE MISSING THE MAIN ISSUE HERE, CHUM, WHICH IS GOOD MANNERS.

YES. YOU'RE RIGHT. QUITE RIGHT. WE'RE NOT AT HOME TO MR. CRUEL HERE. WE APOLOGIZE!
GOOD. THAT'S ALL RIGHT THEN...
...S'GOT A BIT WARM, HASN'T IT?
HA! HIS ELECTRO-MAGNETIC READINGS ARE WILD! SHIFTING, CONSTANTLY. SO... COLORFUL.

HE'S GREY. HE'S SO GREY HE SNUCK ON THE TARDIS WITHOUT ANYONE NOTICING. EVEN HIM!
THERE'S A REASON FOR THAT.
HE'S AN ABERRATION. HIS CELLS. SOMETHING'S STRANGE THERE. THE WAY THEY REACT TO LIGHT. CONSTANTLY CHANGING. IT'S LIKE THE WORLD DOESN'T NOTICE HIM. YET.

"THAT'S HIS TALENT, ALICE. JOHN JONES? HE'S A CHAMELEON."
OO, LOOK. BIG SNAKE...
...IN HACKNEY.

ALLLLRIGHT! COME ON! WE'RE HERE IN THE HOME OF THE DELTA BLUES. THE HEARTLAND OF WHAT WOULD EVENTUALLY BECOME ROCK'N'ROLL AND *DEFINITELY* NOT POLKA!
WE'RE HERE TO SEE ONE OF THE PIONEERS OF ROCK'N'ROLL ITSELF... ROBERT JOHNSON!
JONES! YOU TOO! I WANT YOU TO SEE ONE OF THE MOST ELECTRIFYING LIVE MUSICAL PERFORMERS *IN THE KNOWN UNIVERSE...*

HELLOOO MISSISSIPPI!!
GIMME THE BLUES!!!

NOT BLUES.
GOLD. GOLD. GOLD.
GOLLLLLLLDDD...

UHH... WHICH PART OF HACKNEY IS THIS, EXACTLY?
DOCTOR! THEY'VE BLOCKED THE DOOR!

SSSSS
HOW BAD...
SSSS
...DO YOU WANT TO BE GOOD?

AT GLOW. IT'S SOME SORT OF ASTY, QUICK FIX LIFE-FORCE ANCEMENT. IT'LL MAKE THEM STRONGER, FASTER.
RIENDLIER?
PROBABLY NOT. IT'S GOING TO BURN OUT THEIR INTERNAL ORGANS RATHER QUICKLY, TOO. THEY'RE ALL GOING TO *DIE* UNLESS I CAN REVERSE IT. SOON.

HOW BAD DO YOU...
OOH, A MANTRA! I LOVE A GOOD MANTRA. ESPECIALLY A CREEPY ONE.
LOOK, EVERYONE! LEAVING THE BUILDING! ELVIS!!!

AND OUT WE GO. YOU FIRST, JONES!
SMASH
OI!

ALICE! GET BACK TO THE TARDIS! AND GET JONES BACK SAFELY!
YOU'RE COMING TOO!
YES! OF COURSE! OF *COURSE* I AM!

RIGHT AFTER I SAVE THESE PEOPLE'S LIVES.
WHATEVER'S DONE THIS TO THEM, THEY DON'T DESERVE TO *DIE* LIKE THI...

...OH NO.
ROBERT JOHNSON.
HOW BAD... DO YOU WANT...

... TO BE GOOD? VERY MUCH. *VERY* MUCH!
WRRRRRRR
SAY *AH*, ROBERT! LET'S HEAR THAT FABULOUS FALSETTO.
COME ON... WHATEVER YOU ARE. LET ME FIND THE REPROGRAMMING FREQUENCY AND REVERSE IT.
THERE'S NO DEVIL INSIDE YOU. SOMEONE'S DONE THIS TO YOU. SOMEONE NOT FROM AROUND HERE...
WHIRRRRRR

COUGH
DOCTOR?
HELLO, ROBERT. ONE WORD FOR YOU..

RUNNN!!!
GET TO THE TARDIS!

AND TAKE THIS TO ALICE! SHE'LL KNOW WHAT TO DO!
GO!!

GO.

COME ON THEN. LET'S GET DOWN TO IT. WHO ARE YOU AND WHAT DO YOU WANT?
AND WHY HAVE YOU DONE THIS TO THESE PEOPLE?

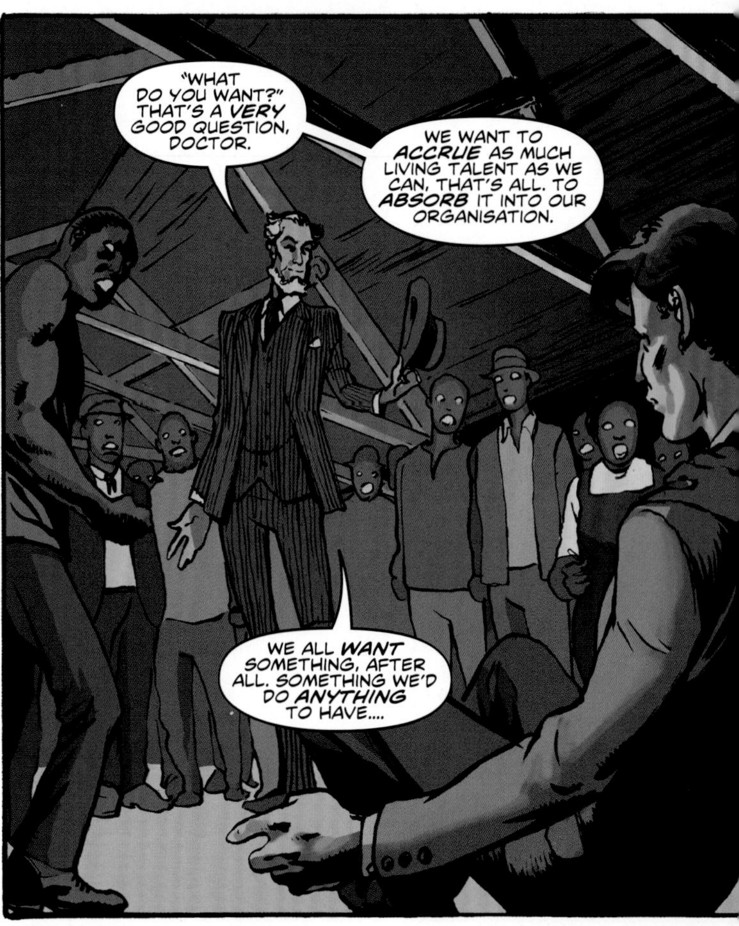
"WHAT DO YOU WANT?" THAT'S A **VERY** GOOD QUESTION, DOCTOR.
WE WANT TO **ACCRUE** AS MUCH LIVING TALENT AS WE CAN, THAT'S ALL. TO **ABSORB** IT INTO OUR ORGANISATION.
WE ALL **WANT** SOMETHING, AFTER ALL. SOMETHING WE'D DO **ANYTHING** TO HAVE....

PERHAPS... SOMETHING YOU'VE LOST?
SERVEYOUINC
THWIP

SERVEYOUINC. YOU LOT AGAIN?
YOU BEING HERE. NOW. THIS ISN'T COINCIDENTAL, IS IT?
NO, DOCTOR. WE BELIEVE YOU'RE SOMEONE WHO COULD **VERY** MUCH ENHANCE OUR ORGANIZATION. AND I'VE BEEN TASKED WITH MAKING YOU AN OFFER YOU **CAN'T** REFUSE.
SERVEYOUINC

SORRY, BIT BUSY AT THE MOMENT **NOT** BEING A MALEVOLENT PRESENCE WILLING TO BURN OUT THE LIFE-FORCE OF INNOCENTS.
I'M NOT SURE I'D REALLY FIT IN TO **YOUR** ORGANIZATION.
COME NOW, DOCTOR. **EVERYONE** HAS A PRICE...

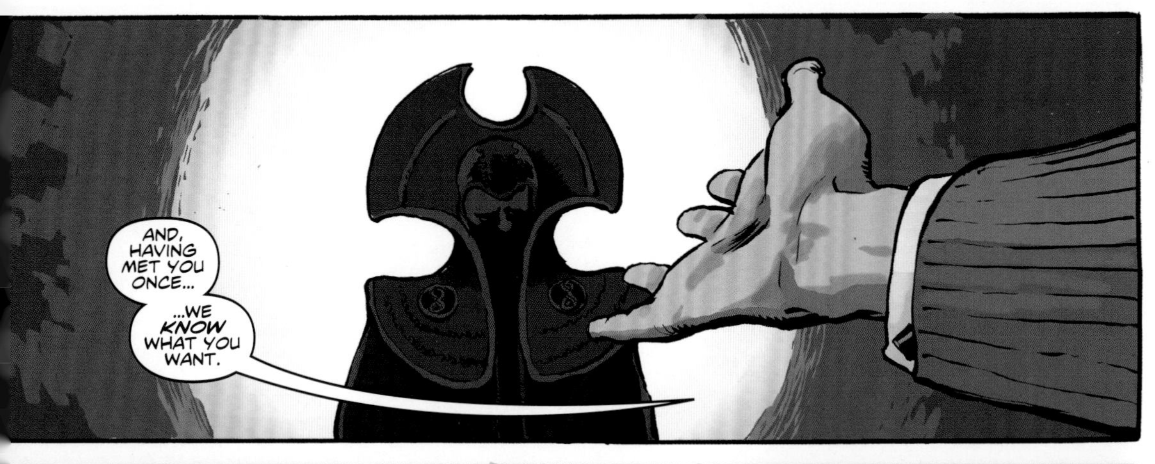
AND, HAVING MET YOU ONCE...
...WE KNOW WHAT YOU WANT.

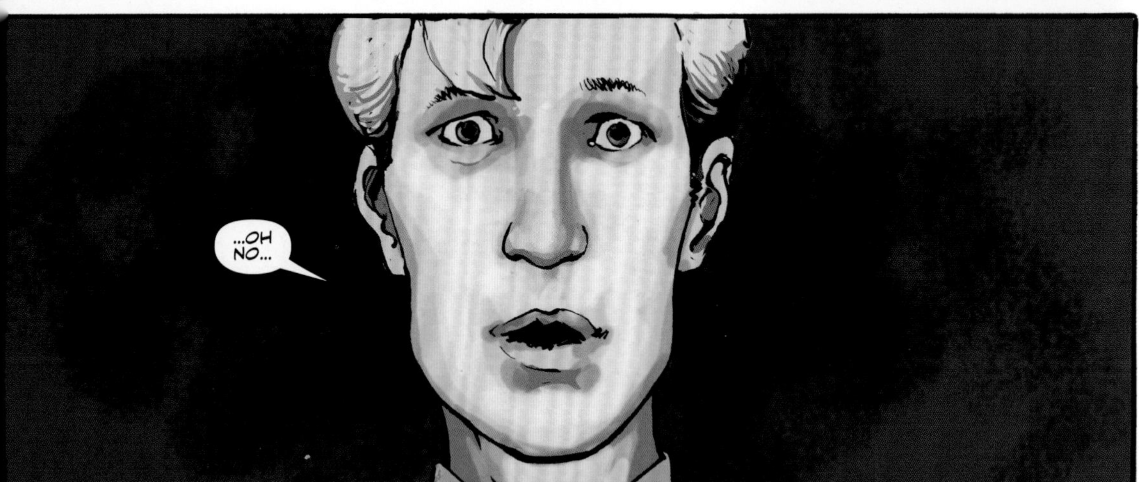
...OH NO...

POLICE PUBLIC CALL BOX
ANYONE IN THERE?
KNOCK KNOCK
DOCTOR TOLD ME TO GIVE THIS THING TO AN ALICE!

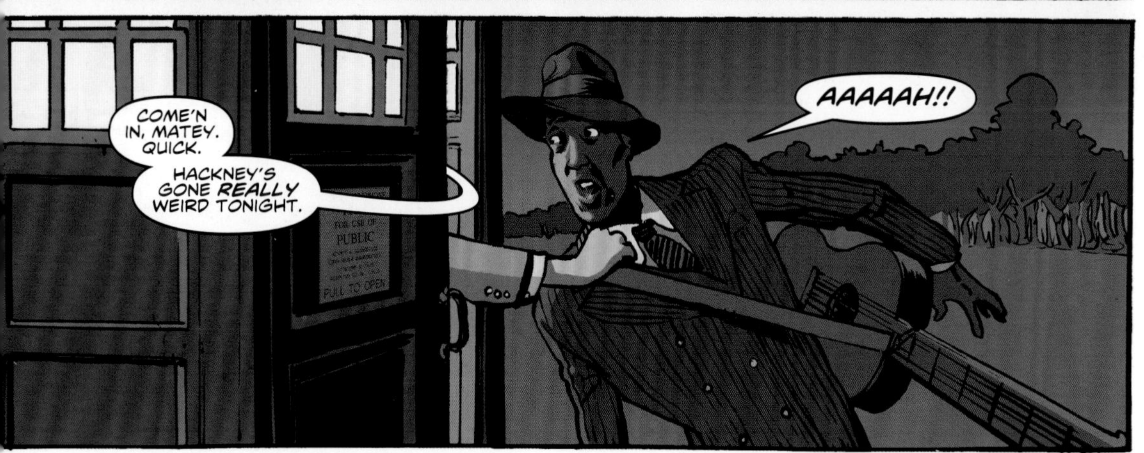
COME'N IN, MATEY. QUICK.
HACKNEY'S GONE REALLY WEIRD TONIGHT.
AAAAAH!!
FOR USE OF PUBLIC
PULL TO OPEN

DAMMIT, BOY. YOU FRIGHTENED THE LIVIN' SOUL OUTTA ME.
HE SNEAKS UP ON PEOPLE. THEY DON'T NOTICE HIM. IT'S A TALENT.
YOU'RE ***ROBERT JOHNSON.*** WHERE'S THE DOCTOR?

THEY GOT HIM.
HE TOLD ME TO GET HIS SCREWDRIVER TO THE ***TARDIS*** AND ALICE. SAID YOU'D KNOW WHAT TO DO.

I'D KNOW WHAT TO DO? I'M NOT A TIME LORD. I'M A LIBRARY ASSISTANT. HOW AM I SUPPOSED TO KNOW WHAT TO DO?
ROBERT JOHNSON. SOLD 'IS SOUL TO THE DEVIL AT THE CROSSROADS IN ORDER TO GAIN A NEAR SUPERNATURAL SKILL ON 'IS GUITAR.
YOU'VE GOT THE SAME NAME. AND YOU'RE A BLUES SINGER.

NO OFFENCE, MATE, BUT YOU NEED TO COME UP WITH A MORE ORIGINAL 'ANDLE.
THAT TALE HAS ACTUALLY BEEN GREATLY EXAGGERATED.
WHAT ***ACTUALLY*** OCCURRED WAS THE DOCTOR GAVE ME 'THE BEST OF ROBERT JOHNSON' FOR MY BIRTHDAY AND THEN...

SHUT UP, YOU TWO!
HE MUST HAVE GIVEN YOU THE SONIC SCREWDRIVER BECAUSE IT WAS IMPORTANT.
HE RELEASED ME FROM MY POSSESSION USING IT.

ALRIGHT. WE'VE PLUGGED THE SONIC INTO THE TARDIS.
YOU'D IMAGINE THAT IT'S DOWNLOADED ITS DATA INTO THE TARDIS' HARD DRIVE. WHATEVER THAT IS. ITS 'MATRIX'.
BUT HOW ARE WE SUPPOSED TO...

RUMMMMBLEEEE

AH...
LOOKS LIKE BESSIE'S READY.
AMPLIFIED...
RUMMMMMMMBLLE

ALRIGHT, YOU TWO...
WE'RE GOING TO GET THE DOCTOR BACK.
AND WE'RE GOING TO USE YOUR TALENTS TO DO IT.

THIS ISN'T HACKNEY, IS IT?
NO, IT'S 1931 MISSISSIPPI, AND YOU'RE CURRENTLY INSIDE A TIME MACHINE. AND THE DOCTOR NEEDS YOU.
I MIGHT MESS THIS UP. I MIGHT BE... RUBBISH.

A MORTAL WITH THE POTENTIAL OF A SUPERMAN... YOU'LL BE SURPRISED AT WHAT YOU DO, JOHN...
THIS IS FROM MY MUM...

MISSISSIPPI, 1931.
NOW.

...THEM.
WE GOT A LITTLE SONG FOR Y'ALL.

NNNNNG
KRA
...CALL IT THE TARDIS BLUES.
BESSIE

TRANNGGGGG
NO!

KRAAAAAANGG

YOU PLUGGED THE SONIC INTO THE TARDIS SO SHE HAD THE REVERSED REPROGRAMMING FREQUENCY.
AND THEN YOU LED THEM ALL *HERE* SO THEY WERE IN THE VICINITY OF A LOCALIZED, INTENSIVE BURST...

...AND YOU USED THE TARDIS, *MY* TARDIS...
...AS AN *AMPLIFIER?*
HELLO, DOCTOR.

I DON'T KNOW. HONESTLY. YOUNG PEOPLE TODAY.
EVERYONE ALRIGHT? I PRESUME YOU ALL JUST HAVE A CRUSHING HEADACHE LIKE ME BUT NO INTERNAL ORGANS EXPLODING.
RAISE YOUR HAND IF YOUR INTERNAL ORGANS ARE CURRENTLY EXPLODING.

LOOKS LIKE EVERYONE'S WELL, DOCTOR. THE DAY IS SAVED!
I SAY THAT CALLS FOR A CELEBRATION!

AND THE PIXIE SMILES AT MEEEEEE...
POLICE PUBLIC CALL BOX

JOHN JONES... HOW YOU MISTREATIN' THAT GUITAR... AND THOSE WORDS YOU SINGIN'.
YOU AND ME'S GONNA HAVE A LONG TALK. AND SOME LESSONS.
YEAH, ALRIGHT...

WELL DONE, CLEVER SARCASTIC LIBRARIAN. YOU CAME BACK FOR ME. THANK YOU.
YOU'RE WELCOME. YOU OKAY?
ME? COURSE, ALICE OBIEFUNE. COURSE I AM.
NO YOU'RE NOT.

...NO I'M NOT.
THEY SHOWED ME SOMETHING, SOMETHING I WANTED SO MUCH THAT IT MADE ME FORGET MYSELF.
...WHAT WAS IT?

THAT'S THE UPSETTING THING...
...I HONESTLY DON'T REMEMBER.

CHAPTER 4 Cover A: Verity Glass

"FIRST OF ALL, WE PROVIDE THE PROPER ENVIRONMENT.
"AN ENCLOSED SYSTEM, WITH ITS OWN ESTABLISHED STRUCTURES AND HEIRARCHIES, WHERE EVERYTHING HAS ITS PLACE..."
"...WHERE EVEN THE STRUGGLES FOR DOMINANCE WITHIN THE SOCIAL ORDER OCCUR INSIDE A STRICTLY DEFINED FRAMEWORK.
"FOR PURPOSES OF DEMONSTRATION..."
UNITED SYSTEM RESEARCH BASE N-DRC/9
...WE'LL BE USING A SMALL COLONY OF TOLUAN SALT-BEETLES.
WE HAVE THE QUEEN HERE, THE FOUR CONSORTS IN THEIR EGG-CHAMBERS THERE, THE SOLDIER-DRONES THERE, AND SO ON.
NOW, SALT-BEETLES ARE AMONG THE MOST NATURALLY INTELLIGENT AND ADAPTABLE SPECIES IN THE GALAXY. SECOND ONLY TO HUMANS, IN FACT.
A HIVE-STRUCTURE LIKE THIS IS MORE THAN CAPABLE OF RESPONDING TO ANY THREAT FROM ITS NATIVE PLANET.
HOWEVER -- NOTICE THE SEALED CAPSULE I'VE PLACED HERE, AT THE HEART OF THE HIVE.
LET'S SEE WHAT HAPPENS...
...WHEN WE INTRODUCE SOMETHING FROM OUTSIDE THEIR FRAME OF REFERENCE.
HMM.

ALL JUST A LITTLE BIT SCHOOL SCIENCE FAIR, ISN'T IT, DR RUTHERFORD?
DO SHUT UP, MELLORS --
HOI!
YOU WILL ADDRESS MR MELLORS AS 'DEPUTY ADMINISTRATOR' OR 'SIR' --
AND YOU CAN SHUT UP TOO, YOU RIDICULOUS MAN. WHY DON'T YOU GO HOVER OVER BALLARD FOR A CHANGE --
ALL RIGHT, ALL RIGHT...
HART -- DON'T CARRY ON SO. WE'RE NOT RUNNING A DICTATORSHIP HERE, ARE WE?
STOUT FELLOW.
...NO, CHIEF CARTWRIGHT.
"SIR."
AND JANET -- RODNEY DOES HAVE A POINT. DOES RESEARCHING BEETLE COLONIES REALLY HAVE ANY SORT OF... AH...
...ANY SORT OF MILITARY APPLICATION? I DO KNOW WHY WE'RE HERE, PETER.
AS YOU CAN SEE, THE COLONY'S NORMAL DEFENCES ARE PROVING USELESS AGAINST THE NEW THREAT.
PUT SIMPLY -- THE BEETLES CANNOT DESTROY WHAT THEY CANNOT UNDERSTAND.
TRANSLATE THAT TO A HUMAN SECURITY SYSTEM AND WE'RE FACED WITH A SIMILAR --
BREEP BREEP BREEP
SORRY. CALL COMING THROUGH.

CHIEF ADMINISTRATOR SPEAKING -- WHAT?
DEAR LORD, YOU'RE NOT SERIOUS. BALLARD TOO?
LOOK, JUST -- STAY THERE AND DON'T TOUCH ANYTHING. I'M ON MY WAY.

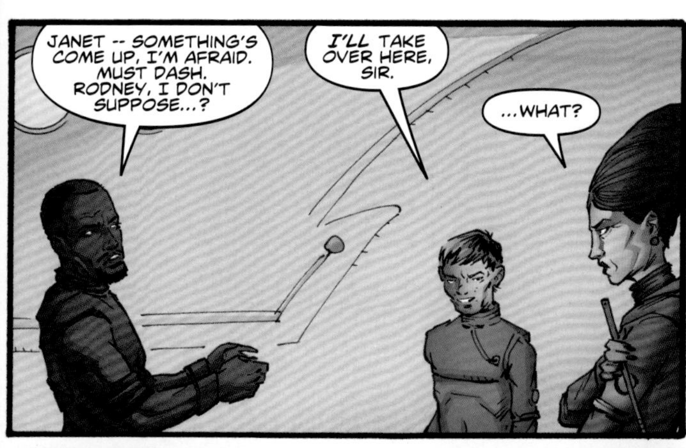
JANET -- SOMETHING'S COME UP, I'M AFRAID. MUST DASH. RODNEY, I DON'T SUPPOSE...?
I'LL TAKE OVER HERE, SIR.
...WHAT?

STOUT FELLOW. HART -- FOLLOW ME.
I'LL JUST NEED A MOMENT HERE, SIR...
PETER, WAIT -- YOU CAN'T JUST --

AND YET, HE HAS -- LEAVING FINAL APPROVAL OF YOUR PROJECT IN MY HANDS...
DON'T BE PIG-HEADED, MELLORS. THIS RESEARCH HAS VITAL IMPLICATIONS FOR --
OH, PLEASE. "YOU CAN'T DESTROY WHAT YOU CAN'T UNDERSTAND?" MS RUTHERFORD...

KRRZZZAKKK
...WHEN YOU CAN DESTROY, YOU DON'T HAVE TO UNDERSTAND.
EXCUSE ME.

I THINK OUR CHIEF OF SECURITY MAKES AN EXCELLENT POINT, DON'T YOU? ANYWAY, YOU'LL HAVE MY REPORT BY THE END OF THE DAY.
I WOULDN'T GET YOUR HOPES UP...
YOU ALRIGHT, DOC?
FWOOSH
OH, DON'T WORRY ABOUT ME, PAMELA.
I'M FINE.
"BUT IF MELLORS WANTS TO THROW HIS WEIGHT AROUND... WELL."
"HE'D JUST BETTER WATCH HIS BACK.
"THAT'S ALL."
HM?
IS SOMEONE...?
OH GOD -- NO! S-STAY BACK -- PLEASE --
SOMEONE! ANYONE! HELP ME! HELP MEEEE -
EEEEAAAAAAAAHHHHH!!

CHAPTER 4

WHODUNNIT?

WRITER
AL EWING

ARTIST
BOO COOK

COLORIST
HI-FI

LETTERER
RICHARD STARKINGS AND COMICRAFT'S JIMMY BETANCOURT

ALICE? WHAT IS IT?
SNFF
NOTHING.
UWAEBUKA OBIEFUNE IJEZIE
BELOVED HUSBAND AND FATHER
"The world is complex do not lose hope"
NO. WHEN SOMETHING IS WRONG, YOU SAY WHAT IT *IS*. DON'T *EVER* KEEP IT TO YOURSELF, UNDERSTAND?
WHEN YOU KEEP IT TO YOURSELF, THE WRONG GOES *ON*.
...*MADDIE POTTER* SAID YOU AND DAD SHOULD GO BACK WHERE YOU *CAME* FROM.
I TOLD HER DAD WAS *DEAD* AND SHE SAID *HER* DAD SAID IT WAS *GOOD RIDDANCE* --
TT!
THAT GIRL *AND* HER FATHER NEED A GOOD SLAP. DID YOU TELL YOUR *TEACHER?*
SHE SAID MADDIE WAS ONLY *TEASING*. SHE *ALWAYS* SAYS THAT. IT'S NOT *FAIR*.
NOTHING'S EVER FAIR.

SOMETIMES I JUST WANNA GO *AWAY*.
GO AWAY INTO *SPACE* AND NOT *EVER* COME BACK.

OH?
AND WHAT HAPPENS TO THE *REST* OF US, THEN?
WHO HAVE TO STAY *BEHIND?*

LA DA DA DUM... DEEDLE-DE-DUM...
POLICE PUBLIC CALL BOX
HELLO BA-BY, I'LL DATE YOU ON MON-DAY, AND NOW FOR SOME WHIM-SY, 'COS I'M OH-SO-CHEE-KY...
CHEEKY AND CHIR-PY, A CHUCKLESOME CHAP-PY, SORT OF A HIP-PY, UNTHREATENING TO YOUR PARENTS IN TERMS OF MY SEXUAL-IT-Y, YEAH!
LAST LINE DOESN'T QUITE SCAN YET, BUT I'M HAPPY WITH IT. NICE AND POPPY, INNIT?
WHAT YOU RECKON? BE BRUTAL.
ALL RIGHT, I SUPPOSE. I MEAN, IT WAS SORT OF SMUG AND BLAND AND A LITTLE CREEPY, BUT... UM... IT WAS...
...COMPETENT?
OH.
COULD YOU BE A BIT LESS BRUTAL?
FIRST RULE, JOHNNY-BOY! NEVER READ THE REVIEWS!
SECOND RULE IS NEVER ADMIT YOU DID READ THE REVIEWS. "VERY RUDE, TASTELESS COAT, TWO STARS." WHICH PLANET-SAVER. I'VE NEVER FORGOTTEN.
THE IMPORTANT THING IS KEEP TRYING, YOU'LL GET THERE EVENTUALLY...
YEAH, AND SPEAKING OF GETTING THERE EVENTUALLY --

-- REMEMBER I HAD THAT SOLICITOR'S APPOINTMENT I NEEDED TO BE BACK IN LONDON FOR?
ABOUT TWO ICE PLANETS AND A DINOSAUR CIVILISATION AGO?
YES, I REMEMBER. BUSINESS WITH YOUR HORRIBLE LANDLORD, WASN'T IT?
YEAH. HOPEFULLY I WON'T HAVE TO TAKE HIM TO COURT, BUT... I DON'T KNOW.
SOUNDS VERY STRESSFUL. AS YOUR DOCTOR, I PRESCRIBE A NICE HOLIDAY.
NOW, THERE'S A RESORT PLANET ORBITING JANGRA IV -- ROTATIONARY WOBBLE MEANS IT'S ALWAYS THE PERFECT SUNSET, AND THEY DO COCKTAILS --
-- SLIGHT CHANCE IT'S BEEN OVERRUN BY KILLER ROBOTS, OBVIOUSLY, BUT THE IMPORTANT THING IS TO RELAX AND HAVE FUN --
DOCTOR!
I CAN'T KEEP RUNNING AWAY FROM MY PROBLEMS!
'COURSE YOU CAN. TIME MACHINE! TAKE A DAY OR TWO. TAKE A WEEK. YOU CAN BE BACK BEFORE YOU EVER LEFT.
DOCTOR, I TOOK A WEEK. A WEEK AGO. I NEED TO GET THIS DONE.
WHAT AM I SUPPOSED TO DO? JUST KEEP RUNNING AWAY FOREVER, IS THAT IT?
...
WELL, IT WORKED FOR ME.

AND FOR A LOT OF OTHER PEOPLE I KNOW, TOO.
SORRY?

THE PEOPLE I TRAVEL WITH. MY COMPANIONS ALONG THE WAY.
I'VE TAKEN ON A LOT OF STRAYS OVER THE YEARS -- STOWAWAYS, LIKE JONES. AND PEOPLE WHO DIDN'T HAVE MUCH TO LEAVE BEHIND.

AND SOMETIMES -- JUST SOMETIMES, MIND YOU -- I GOT TO LEAVE THEM SOMEWHERE BETTER THAN I FOUND THEM.
SORT OF TOOK THE STING OUT OF THE WHOLE INEVITABLE GOODBYE THING --
AND THAT'S WHAT I AM, IS IT? A STRAY?

SOMEONE WITH NOTHING, SOMEONE YOU CAN JUST -- JUST FIND A HOME FOR? DO YOU EVER LISTEN TO YOURSELF?
I DIDN'T MEAN --
REMEMBER WHAT YOU SAID THE DAY WE MET? HOW YOU DON'T KEEP PETS? YOU MAKE FRIENDS?

EXCEPT USUALLY THEY'RE THE SAME THING.
IS THAT WHAT I AM, THEN? IS THAT WHAT ALL YOUR "COMPANIONS" ARE TO YOU? IS THAT WHAT WE'RE FOR?
DO YOU EVEN KNOW?

...LET'S GET YOU HOME.
YEAH.
LET'S.

VWOORRRP VWOORRRP
OH, ARE WE GOING TO YOUR PLACE? MIND IF I USE YOUR TOILET?
KNOCK YOURSELF OUT.
...AND THERE WE GO.
POLICE

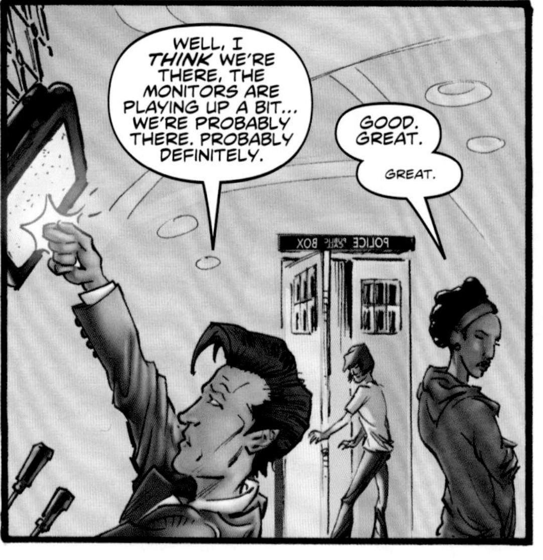
WELL, I THINK WE'RE THERE, THE MONITORS ARE PLAYING UP A BIT... WE'RE PROBABLY THERE. PROBABLY DEFINITELY.
GOOD. GREAT.
GREAT.

ALICE?
OH, FOR --

TOILET'S THE SECOND DOOR ON THE --
OH.
POLICE TELEPHONE
FREE
FOR USE OF
PUBLIC
ADVICE & ASSISTANCE OBTAINABLE IMMEDIATELY
OFFICER & CARS
THIS... THIS *IS* YOUR FLAT, YEAH?
POLICE BOX
HAVE YOU *REDECORATED?*
ON MY SIGNAL!
IF THEY MAKE A MOVE TO *RESIST* -- *KILL THEM!*

MOVE AWAY FROM THE BLUE BOX. HANDS BEHIND YOUR HEADS.
WHO'S THIS, THEN? FRIEND OF YOURS?
NOT LIKELY. HIS NAME'S HART -- WE'VE MET HIM BEFORE. OR AFTER, MAYBE.
BASICALLY HIS JOB IS TO POINT GUNS AT PEOPLE AND SHOUT A LOT --
QUIET!
SEE?
HOW DID YOU KNOW MY NAME? DID YOU CAUSE THE BREACH?
WHAT'S THIS MACHINE YOU ARRIVED IN, SOME SORT OF TELEPORTER?
IT'S CALLED THE TARDIS.
IT'S A MAGICAL BOX MADE OF ADVENTURES. I'D EXPLAIN FURTHER BUT YOU'D ONLY WANT TO MAKE A GUN OUT OF IT.
NOW, AS FOR HOW WE KNOW YOUR NAME --
POLIC NE
FOR USE OF
PUBLIC
ADVICE & ASSISTANCE
OBTAINABLE IMMEDIATELY
OFFICERS & CARS
RESPOND TO ALL CALLS
PULL TO OPEN
HANDS! BEHIND! YOUR HEAD!
-- I'M GOING TO VERY, VERY SLOWLY REACH INTO MY JACKET POCKET. WITHOUT GETTING SHOT.
BECAUSE I DON'T KEEP WEAPONS IN HERE, NOT EVEN SCREWDRIVERS, ALL I HAVE...
...IS A PIECE OF PAPER.

HMMPH.
WEAPONS DOWN, MEN.
THE INSPECTOR, HERE --

I PREFER "THE DOCTOR", THANKS.
-- IS APPARENTLY GOING TO SHOW US ALL HOW A MURDER INVESTIGATION IS RUN.
YES! THAT'S RIGHT. I'M TAKING OVER THIS...

...MURDER MYSTERY.
OOH. MUST BE MY BIRTHDAY.
POLICE PUBLIC CALL BOX
AND WHO ARE THESE TWO, "DOCTOR"? YOUR INTERNS?

I AM NOT HIS INTERN --
AUGUST HART, MEET ALICE OBIEFUNE. SHE'S AN INFORMATION STORAGE AND RETRIEVAL SPECIALIST.
OR ASSISTANT SPECIALIST. I'M ALWAYS GETTING IT WRONG.

AND JONES IS... JONES... IS... AH...
...AN INTERN.
BUT WE EXPECT GREAT THINGS FROM HIM!
OH LOOK, THERE'S FLIES.
FLIES FROM THE STARS.
I'LL CALL MY NEXT BAND THAT.

HULLO.
CHARMED.
DOCTOR? A WORD?

PSYCHIC PAPER. PEOPLE SEE WHATEVER HIGHER AUTHORITY THEY EXPECT TO, LETS YOU IN ANYWHERE. FAKE I.D. MEETS SKELETON KEY.
POLICE PUBLIC CALL BOX
NOT WHAT I WAS GOING TO ASK.
YOU SAID WE WERE HOME. MY HOME.

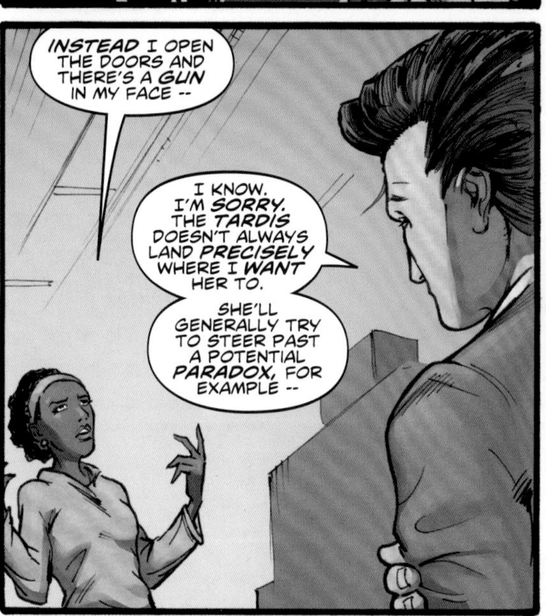
INSTEAD I OPEN THE DOORS AND THERE'S A GUN IN MY FACE --
I KNOW. I'M SORRY. THE TARDIS DOESN'T ALWAYS LAND PRECISELY WHERE I WANT HER TO.
SHE'LL GENERALLY TRY TO STEER PAST A POTENTIAL PARADOX, FOR EXAMPLE --

LIKE HART MEETING US BEFORE WE MET HIM, YOU MEAN?
RIGHT. IF FOR SOME REASON THAT FUTURE MEETING, THIS ONE WE'RE HAVING NOW, DIDN'T HAPPEN -- THAT WOULD BE A PARADOX.
SO IF, SAY, YOU WERE TO STOP TRAVELING IN THE TARDIS... BEFORE WE... WE...

DOCTOR? WHEN YOU'RE QUITE FINISHED...
...YES, OF COURSE.
JUST COMING.

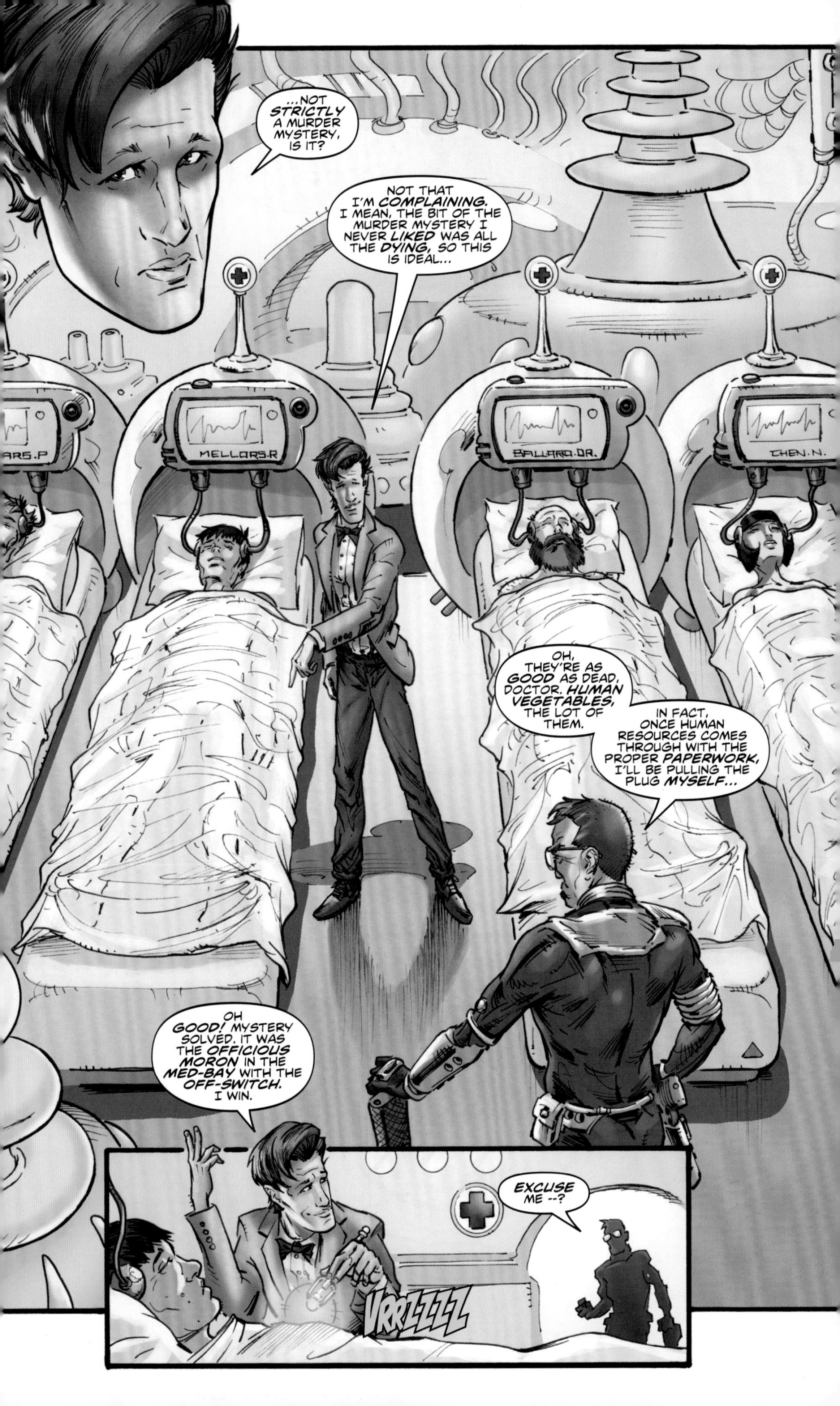
...NOT STRICTLY A MURDER MYSTERY, IS IT?
NOT THAT I'M COMPLAINING. I MEAN, THE BIT OF THE MURDER MYSTERY I NEVER LIKED WAS ALL THE DYING, SO THIS IS IDEAL...
MELLORS.R
BALLARD.DR.
CHEN.N.
OH, THEY'RE AS GOOD AS DEAD, DOCTOR. HUMAN VEGETABLES, THE LOT OF THEM.
IN FACT, ONCE HUMAN RESOURCES COMES THROUGH WITH THE PROPER PAPERWORK, I'LL BE PULLING THE PLUG MYSELF...
OH GOOD! MYSTERY SOLVED. IT WAS THE OFFICIOUS MORON IN THE MED-BAY WITH THE OFF-SWITCH. I WIN.
EXCUSE ME --?
VRRZZZZ

SONIC SCREWDRIVER. PUTS UP SHELVES, OPENS MOST DOORS, MAKES A NICE REMOTE FOR THE TELLY. ALSO DETECTS BRAIN ACTIVITY.
THERE'S NOTHING WRONG WITH ANY OF THESE PEOPLE.
I SERVED IN THE WHEEL WARS, DOCTOR. I'VE SEEN MEN IN COMAS BEFORE --
THIS ISN'T A COMA. NOT AN ORDINARY ONE, ANYWAY.
TELL ME HOW YOU FOUND THEM.
NOT MUCH TO TELL, REALLY. DOCTOR BALLARD AND HIS PEOPLE WERE IN ONE OF THE RESTRICTED LABS -- MELLORS, THE ADMINISTRATOR, WAS IN A CORRIDOR.
ALL OF THEM, FOUND LIKE THIS -- BARELY CLINGING TO LIFE. NO RESPONSE TO STIMULI.
BUT PLEASE, TELL ME MORE ABOUT HOW THERE'S NOTHING WRONG...
IMAGINE A HARD DRIVE. YOU MOVE ALL YOUR FILES OFF IT, EVERY SINGLE ONE, AND SUDDENLY YOUR COMPUTER DOESN'T WORK ANYMORE.
NOTHING WRONG WITH THE HARDWARE. JUST THE INFORMATION. PUT IT ALL BACK, AND YOU'RE FINE.
ONE MORE QUESTION, THOUGH.
IF YOU'RE CALLING THIS MURDER...
WHODUNNIT?

WELL, AFTER IT GOT MELLORS WE SEALED THE ENTIRE LABORATORY WING.
THAT'S RIGHT, DEADLOCKED. SO AT LEAST WE KNOW IT'S CONTAINED. BUT...
...WELL, I THINK BALLARD MIGHT HAVE BEEN HOLDING BACK.
P. CARTWRIGHT DEPUTY ADMINISTRATOR
EXACTLY. EITHER MAKING HIMSELF INDISPENSABLE OR SAVING THE GOOD STUFF FOR OUR COMPETITORS.
WHAT I'M SAYING, MR THORNE, IS THAT WE DON'T REALLY KNOW WHAT THE ARC CAN DO.
AND NOW APPARENTLY THERE'S SOME INSPECTOR COME FROM THE BLOODY MINISTRY OF SCIENCE POKING HIS NOSE IN...
YES, SIR, WE HAVE A COVER STORY IN PLACE. JANET RUTHERFORD -- YES, TERRIBLE SHAME, BUT SOMEONE HAS TO TAKE THE...
DOOR OPEN
SORRY, SOMEONE'S AT THE DOOR.
YOU'RE SUPPOSED TO KNOCK --
::::
OH. OH DEAR LORD.
::::
IT GOT OUT.

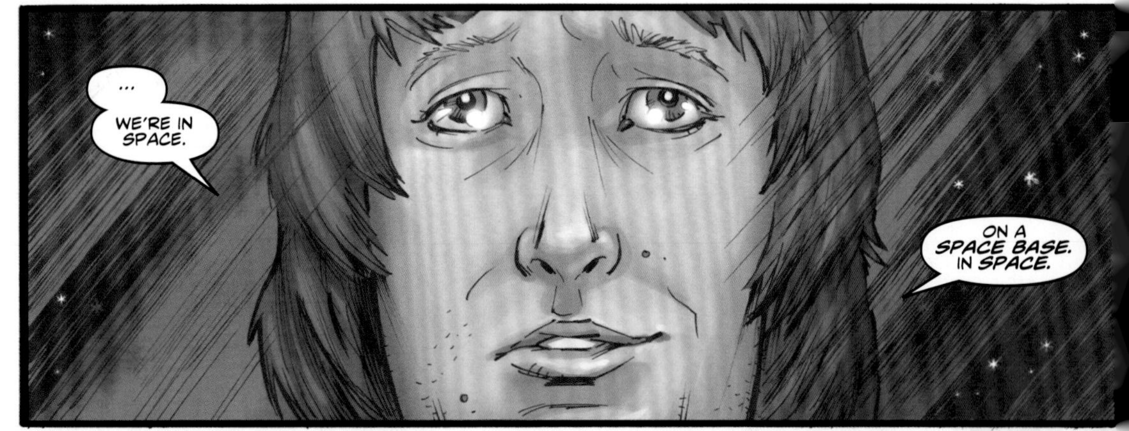
...
WE'RE IN SPACE.
ON A SPACE BASE. IN SPACE.

FAR OUT.
YOU FLEW HERE IN AN ACTUAL TIME MACHINE, JONES. WHAT ARE YOU SO EXCITED NOW FOR?
NO WINDOWS ON THE TARDIS, ARE THERE?
IT'S LIKE YOU'RE JUST... I DUNNO, IN A ROOM. IT'S A REALLY GROOVY PSYCHEDELIC PAD AND ALL, BUT... YEAH, IT'S A ROOM.
Major TOM 2-D PIES
COLLECT
VITA BURSST
PRO TEEN PILZ

BUT HERE... LOOKING OUT THAT WINDOW... IT'S LIKE...
LIKE I'M SITTING IN A TIN CAN, FAR ABOVE THE WORLD...

AND PLANET EARTH IS ALL SMALL AND... WELL, SORT OF ORANGE...
THAT'S NOT PLANET EARTH, JONES.
NOT-PLANET-EARTH IS ORANGE, AND THERE'S NOTHING I CAN RHYME WITH ORANGE...

DUM DA DUM DA DUM... DA DUM DUM...
HERE. HAVE A PROTEIN PILL.
DON'T MIND IF I DO.
SO WHAT'S UP WITH YOU THEN?
PRO TEEN PILZ

'CAUSE LATELY YOU LOOK LIKE YOU'VE BEEN SUCKING ON LEMON PILLS.
I SHOULD TAKE A LEMON PILL. DON'T WANT TO GET SPACE SCURVY.
OH, I DON'T KNOW... NO, I DO KNOW. IT'S THE DOCTOR.
NEW CHUNKY DORIES

I KNOW HE MEANS WELL. HE'S REALLY SWEET, SOMETIMES. BUT...
... I'M NOT GOING TO BE HIS RESCUE ANIMAL, JOHN. AND I CAN'T STAY ON THE TARDIS FOREVER. I JUST CAN'T.
IT'S NOT HOW I WAS RAISED.

IT'S A HARD WORLD, ALICE. VERY HARD AND VERY CRUEL.
BUT YOU CAN'T RUN AWAY FROM IT AND LEAVE THE REST OF US TO DEAL WITH THE MADDIE POTTERS.
YOU HAVE TO STAY AND FIGHT.

UM. HAVE YOU HAD A LOOK ROUND THIS PLACE?
YEAH, I KNOW. ORANGE PLANETS.
IT IS BEAUTIFUL. AND I DON'T WANT TO GIVE ALL THIS UP, I REALLY DON'T. BUT IF HE'S MAKING IT A CHOICE...

NO, I MEANT HAVE YOU SEEN A TOILET ANYWHERE? I'VE STILL NOT BEEN --
BACK DOWN THE CORRIDOR. SECOND ON YOUR LEFT.
HAVE FUN.

HAVING FUN, ARE WE?
COME TO GLOAT?
OUR CHIEF SUSPECT.
DR RUTHERFORD WAS HEARD MAKING THREATS AGAINST MELLORS BEFORE HE ENTERED HIS COMA -- OR WHATEVER YOU WANT TO CALL IT.
AND WITH DOCTOR BALLARD'S TEAM OUT OF THE WAY, HER PROJECTS WOULD GET PRIORITY -- AND FUNDING.
ANYWAY, I ASSUME YOU'LL BE FOLLOWING PROTOCOL AND TAKING HER AWAY FOR INTERROGATION --
I'M FEELING SPONTANEOUS TODAY. LET'S DO THE INTERROGATION RIGHT HERE.
BECAUSE I'VE GOT JUST ONE QUESTION FOR YOU, DR RUTHERFORD...
JUST HOW STUPID DO YOU SUPPOSE HART THINKS I AM?
OH!
VRRZZZZ
K-CHAK

HOW DARE YOU! THAT IS A CLEAR BREACH OF STANDARD OPERATING --
BREACH! NOW WHERE HAVE I HEARD THAT WORD BEFORE?
OH WAIT, IT WAS WHEN YOU WERE THREATENING MY FRIENDS. "DID YOU CAUSE THE BREACH," YOU ASKED.

BREACH OF WHAT? BREACH OF SECURITY? BREACH OF CONTAINMENT?
I DON'T HAVE TO EXPLAIN MYSELF TO YOU --
NO, YOU'D RATHER SWITCH OFF ALL THE WITNESSES AND DISTRACT THE AUTHORITIES WITH A HANDY SCAPEGOAT.

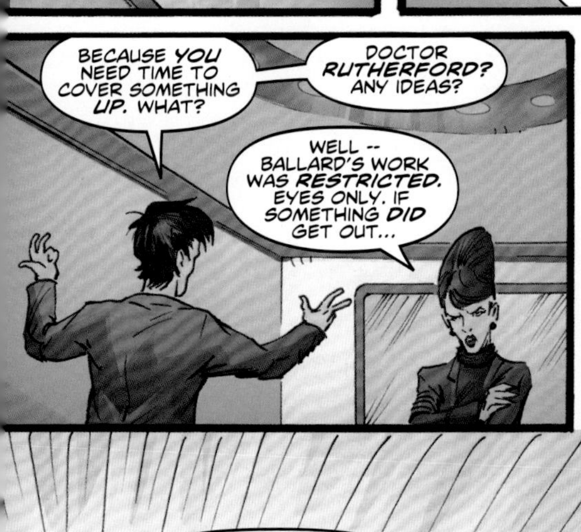
BECAUSE YOU NEED TIME TO COVER SOMETHING UP. WHAT?
DOCTOR RUTHERFORD? ANY IDEAS?
WELL -- BALLARD'S WORK WAS RESTRICTED. EYES ONLY. IF SOMETHING DID GET OUT...

...IT MIGHT BE SOMETHING CARTWRIGHT AND HIS SUPERIORS DON'T WANT THE MINISTRY OF SCIENCE KNOWING ABOUT.
...SUPERIORS?
THE CORPORATION THAT RUNS THIS FACILITY, DOCTOR.

SERVEYOU INC.
AND NOW YOU KNOW TOO MUCH...

AND I THINK THIS TOILET KNOWS WHICH WAY TO *FLOW...*
AND I'VE WIPED MY BOTTOM VERY MUCH --
"WE ***KNOOOOW!***"

MISSION CONTROL TO COLONEL JOHN, PLEASE ***WASH YOUR HANDS,*** YOU'VE ***TOUCHED YOUR BUM,*** CAN YOU ***HEAR*** ME COLONEL JOHN...
MAYBE I SHOULD MAKE IT A BIT LESS TOILET-Y.
::::

...HELLO?
DOES SOMEONE WANT TO USE THE...
EMPTY
:: ::
OH.
OH, ***WOW.***

:: ARC ::
:: ARC ::
...DO YOU PLAY GUITAR?

CHAPTER 5

Cover A: Verity Glass

:: ::
OH. OH, WOW.
EMPTY
:: ARC ::
:: ARC ::
...DO YOU PLAY GUITAR?
EMPTY
JONES!
MOVE!
:: ? ::

FWOOOOSSSHHH
FWASSSHHH
WHILE IT'S BLIND -- HEAD TOWARDS THE SOUND OF MY VOICE!
DON'T LET IT TOUCH YOU!

:: SSSS ::
:: SSSSOO ::
HERE I AM!
WHAT DO YOU THINK IT'S DOING -?
RIGHT NOW? NOT KILLING YOU.
COME ON, JONES -- WE NEED TO GET OUT OF HERE--
YOU NEVER KNOW.
MAYBE IT WANTED TO BE FRIENDS.
:: SSOOOO ::
:: NNNN ::
:: SOOUNNNND ::
:: THEHHH ::
:: SOUND ::
:: THE SOUND ::
:: OF MY ::
:: VOOOICE ::

INTERROGATIO
THIS ISN'T GOING TO BE SO EASY TO EXPLAIN, CHIEF SECURITY OFFICER HART.
YOUR DEATH, DOCTOR? OH, I THINK I'LL FIND A WAY. PERHAPS YOU'RE IN LEAGUE WITH RUTHERFORD HERE.
TWO SPIES TOGETHER, TRYING TO SABOTAGE DOCTOR BALLARD'S GREAT WORK.
WHATEVER YOUR MOTIVES... YOU JUST MADE A DESPERATE LUNGE FOR MY WEAPON. THAT ONE'S AS OLD AS TIME.
AND THEN... I HAD NO CHOICE BUT TO SHOOT Y--
NO, NO, NO!
NOT THAT!
THIS!
VVVWWWWW
SPAK
AAARRGGHH -

CHAPTER 5

THE SOUND OF OUR VOICES

WRITER
AL EWING

ARTIST
BOO COOK

COLORIST
HI-FI

LETTERER
RICHARD STARKINGS AND COMICRAFT'S JIMMY BETANCOURT

'COS IF I WANTED TO EXPLAIN WHAT I DID THEN, I'D HAVE TO USE BIG WORDS LIKE 'SONIC SCREWDRIVER' AND 'HARMONIC RESONANCE' AND 'COUNTERFREQUENCY'.
AND -- LET'S BE HONEST -- I'D LOSE YOU.
RRRRR--
I DON'T NEED A GUN--
NO, PROBABLY NOT, NOT WITH ME, NOT REALLY A FIGHTER.
MORE OF A RUN-AWAY-ER.
RUN AWAY AND SOLVE THE UNDERLYING PROBLEM, THAT'S MORE MY STYLE.
SO WHAT'S YOUR PROBLEM, CHIEF-SECURITY-OFFICER-AUGUST-HART?
WHAT'S SO BIG AND IMPORTANT AND SCARY THAT YOU'RE ALL PUFFED UP LIKE A THREATENED FISH? EH?
WHAT ARE YOU TRYING TO HIDE?
I'LL KILL YOU--
YOU KNOW, I DON'T THINK YOU'RE VERY NICE, OFFICER HART.
MIND YOUR HEAD.
WHAT?

KRAKK

OH MY GOD! I -- I'VE KILLED HIM!
OH, I SHOULDN'T WORRY, TEN YEARS FROM NOW HE'S FINE...

CLIK CLAK
THERE WE GO, SHOULD KEEP HIM BUSY.

NOW, DOCTOR RUTHERFORD, I HAVE A QUESTION. WHAT WAS THIS GREAT WORK DOCTOR BALLARD WAS GREAT-WORKING ON?
I -- I DON'T KNOW.
UNNH...

SHALL WE FIND OUT?

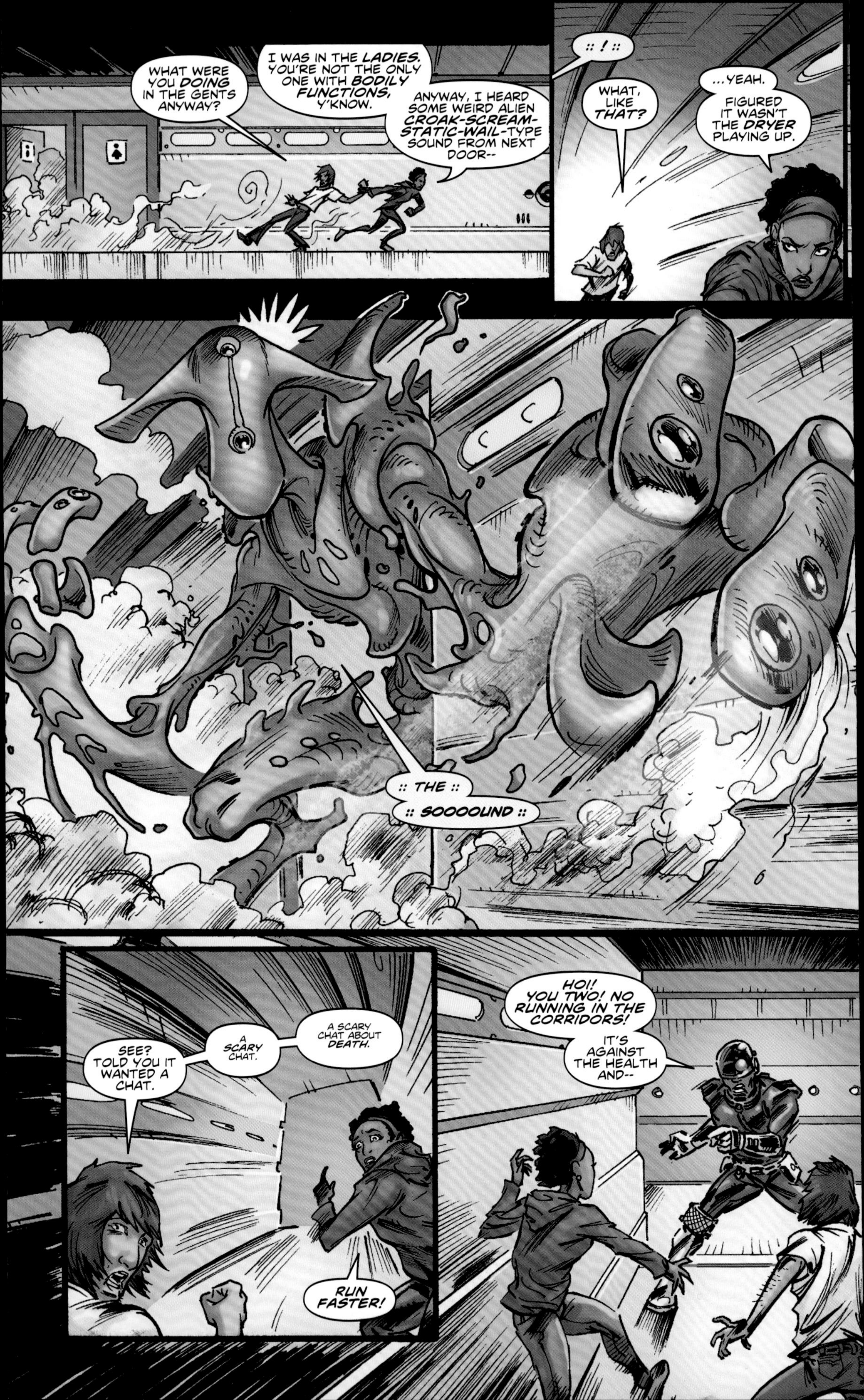
WHAT WERE YOU DOING IN THE GENTS ANYWAY?
I WAS IN THE LADIES. YOU'RE NOT THE ONLY ONE WITH BODILY FUNCTIONS, Y'KNOW.
ANYWAY, I HEARD SOME WEIRD ALIEN CROAK-SCREAM-STATIC-WAIL-TYPE SOUND FROM NEXT DOOR--
:: ! ::
WHAT, LIKE THAT?
...YEAH.
FIGURED IT WASN'T THE DRYER PLAYING UP.
:: THE ::
:: SOOOOUND ::
SEE? TOLD YOU IT WANTED A CHAT.
A SCARY CHAT.
A SCARY CHAT ABOUT DEATH.
RUN FASTER!
HOI! YOU TWO! NO RUNNING IN THE CORRIDORS!
IT'S AGAINST THE HEALTH AND--

-- SAFETY...
:: ARC ::
NO --
NNNNUUHHH --
WHUMP
:: NO ::
:: RUNNING ::

GET A MOVE ON, DAMN YOU!
DIDN'T YOU HEAR ME YELLING?
YES, SIR, SORRY, SIR--
ITS JUST THE INTERROGATION ROOM'S SOUNDPROOFED, SIR, IN CASE OF AN INTERROGATION GETTING OUT OF HAND, SIR, SO--
YES, YES...
JUST GET ME CHIEF ADMINISTRATOR CARTWRIGHT. WE'VE BEEN INFILTRATED.
I WON'T BUY THIS 'MAN FROM THE MINISTRY' STORY ONE SECOND LONGER. THIS 'DOCTOR' IS CLEARLY A CORPORATE SPY.
HE'S BEEN WORKING WITH RUTHERFORD THIS WHOLE TIME --
SIR?
BEGGING YOUR PARDON, SIR, THOUGHT YOU KNEW, SIR.
HE'S BEEN GOT, SIR. LIKE THE OTHERS. IN A COMA, SIR.
...DEAR GOD. REALLY?
BUT THAT MEANS...
...THAT MEANS OPERATIONAL CONTROL OF THE STATION FALLS TO ME.
GOOD.
VERY GOOD.

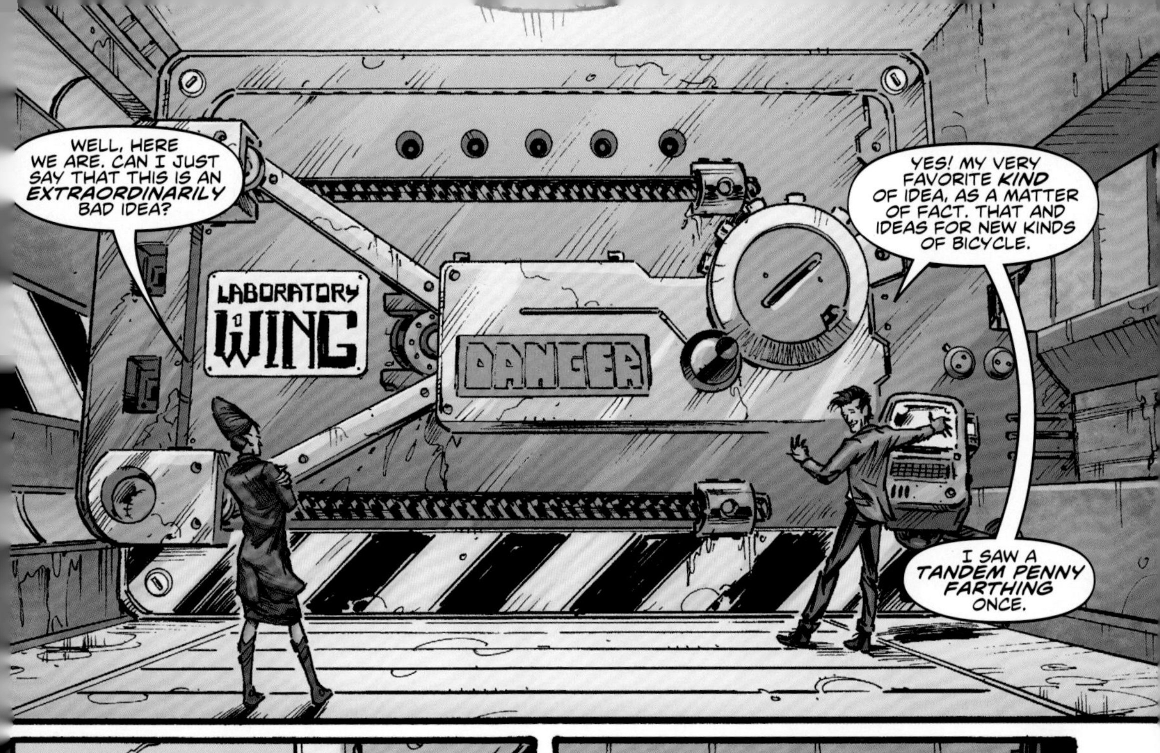
WELL, HERE WE ARE. CAN I JUST SAY THAT THIS IS AN EXTRAORDINARILY BAD IDEA?
LABORATORY WING
DANGER
YES! MY VERY FAVORITE KIND OF IDEA, AS A MATTER OF FACT. THAT AND IDEAS FOR NEW KINDS OF BICYCLE.
I SAW A TANDEM PENNY FARTHING ONCE.

YES, WELL... FOR ONE THING, WHATEVER ATTACKED MELLORS AND THE OTHERS IS PROBABLY STILL IN THERE.
FOR ANOTHER... I DON'T THINK EVEN YOUR GADGET CAN GET THROUGH THIS.

SOLID TITANIUM, PROTECTED BY A TENTH-GENERATION QUANTUM-LIQUID--
-- DEADLOCK SEAL ENCRYPTION, YES.
ABSOLUTELY POSITIVELY IMPOSSIBLE TO GET THROUGH...
VVVWWWW

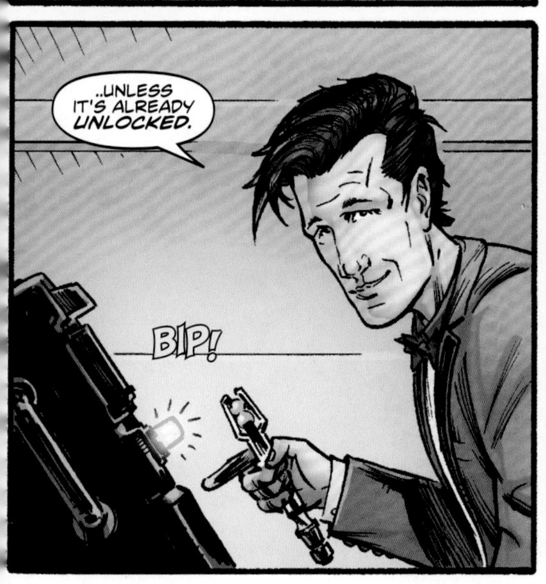
..UNLESS IT'S ALREADY UNLOCKED.
BIP!

WHICH MEANS SOMEONE UNLOCKED IT FROM THE INSIDE. SOMEONE WHO KNEW THE PASS CODE.
BUT IT WAS EVACUATED -- THERE WEREN'T ANY PEOPLE IN THERE --
WEREN'T THERE?
LET'S SEE.

BALLARD'S LABORATORY...
HMM. LET'S DO A LITTLE THOUGHT EXERCISE, DOCTOR RUTHERFORD.
WHAT DO YOU SEE?
WELL... BEAR IN MIND THIS IS THE FIRST TIME I'VE SEEN HIS SETUP, BUT...
THAT'S DEFINITELY A CONTAINMENT CUBE -- A FORCE FIELD FOR HOLDING SOME SORT OF DANGEROUS SPECIMEN.
JUDGING BY THE BURNED-OUT POWER CELLS, THE FIELD FAILED, OR WAS BREACHED...
WHAT ABOUT THE SHARP POINTY THINGS?
PROBE UNITS, DESIGNED TO PENETRATE THE FIELD. SET TO DELIVER STIMULUS -- ELECTRIC SHOCK, MOST LIKELY -- THEN RECORD THE RESULT.
IT'S A TESTING FACILITY. OR IT WAS.
WHY? WHAT DO YOU SEE?
A TORTURE CHAMBER.

QUITE AN EMOTIONAL WAY OF PUTTING IT, DOCTOR. TESTS MUST BE CONDUCTED...
YES, MY THOUGHTS EXACTLY.
YOU FAIL.

F MINUS MINUS, RUTHERFORD, MUST TRY HARDER.
EXCUSE ME?
THAT'S WHAT HAPPENS WHEN YOU DON'T SEE PEOPLE.

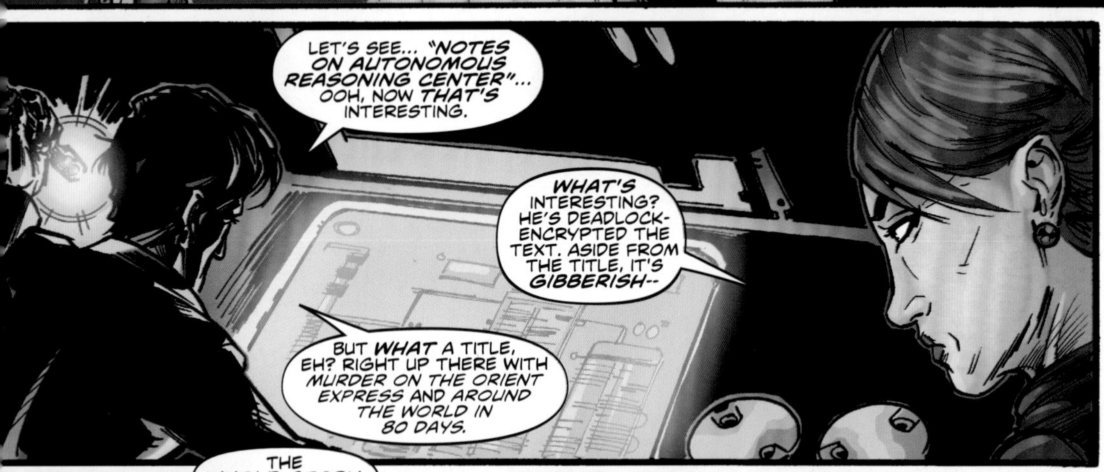
LET'S SEE... "NOTES ON AUTONOMOUS REASONING CENTER"... OOH, NOW THAT'S INTERESTING.
WHAT'S INTERESTING? HE'S DEADLOCK-ENCRYPTED THE TEXT. ASIDE FROM THE TITLE, IT'S GIBBERISH--
BUT WHAT A TITLE, EH? RIGHT UP THERE WITH MURDER ON THE ORIENT EXPRESS AND AROUND THE WORLD IN 80 DAYS.

THE WHOLE STORY, ENCAPSULATED.
OH, WE'RE MISSING DETAILS, BUT RIGHT THERE WE HAVE THE HOW, THE WHAT, AND MOST IMPORTANTLY...
...THE WHO.

WHICH JUST LEAVES US WITH THE WHY.
TO BE CONTINUED.

JONES, COME ON!
HOW COME A FORTY-YEAR-OLD LIBRARY ASSISTANT IS FASTER ON HER FEET THAN A TWENTY-YEAR-OLD ROCK STAR?
ROCK STAR?
YOU'RE FROM THE SIXTIES! BEFORE VIDEO GAMES AND TURKEY TWIZZLERS!
I -- HUFF -- I GOT A STITCH--
JUST KEEP GOING! WE'LL BE SAFE IF WE CAN GET TO THE--
HANGAR 18
-- TARDIS...
POLICE PUBLIC CALL
AH, MS... OBIEFUNE, WAS IT? AND THE OTHER ONE, AS WELL.
NOW ALL WE NEED IS THE DOCTOR, AND WE CAN CLEAR UP THIS WHOLE UNFORTUNATE MESS.
I'M SURE ONCE HE HEARS YOUR SCREAMS, HE'LL COME RUNNING.
KNEECAPS, GENTLEMEN. THE BOY FIRST.
OR --

-- YOU COULD USE THE PA SYSTEM.
"PAGING THE DOCTOR, PLEASE COME TO THE WHITE COURTESY PHONE," THAT SORT OF THING.
MUCH MORE CIVILIZED THAN "OW, ARGH, MY KNEECAP".

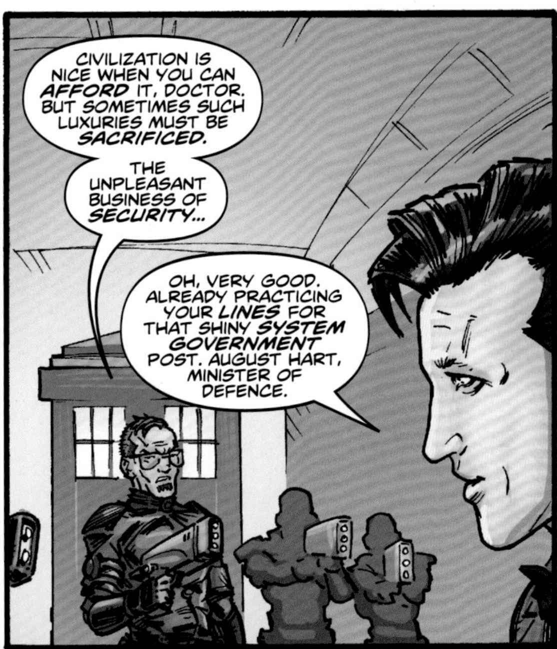
CIVILIZATION IS NICE WHEN YOU CAN AFFORD IT, DOCTOR. BUT SOMETIMES SUCH LUXURIES MUST BE SACRIFICED.
THE UNPLEASANT BUSINESS OF SECURITY...
OH, VERY GOOD. ALREADY PRACTICING YOUR LINES FOR THAT SHINY SYSTEM GOVERNMENT POST. AUGUST HART, MINISTER OF DEFENCE.

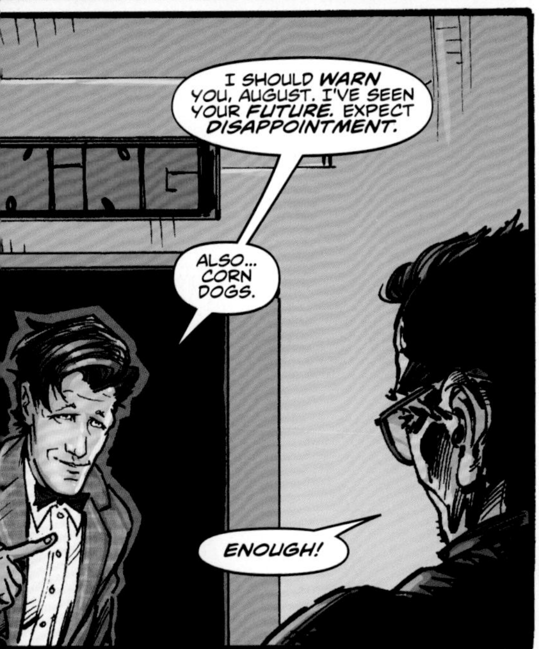
I SHOULD WARN YOU, AUGUST. I'VE SEEN YOUR FUTURE. EXPECT DISAPPOINTMENT.
ALSO... CORN DOGS.
ENOUGH!

YOU HAVE FIVE WEAPONS TRAINED ON YOU, DOCTOR. REACH FOR YOUR... GADGET... AND THEY WILL FIRE.
WHAT'S YOUR REAL PURPOSE HERE?
OH, NOTHING MUCH. THOUGHT I'D USE THE TARDIS CONSOLE TO TRACK SOMEONE DOWN, THAT'S ALL.
BUT JUDGING BY JONES AND ALICE'S GENERAL DISCOMBOBULATION...

HE'S ALREADY HERE.
WELL? COME ON OUT, THEN! NOBODY'S GOING TO HURT YOU!

:: ::
:: ARC ::
:: ARC ::
LORD ABOVE--
ON MY SIGNAL!
AIM AND--
POLICE PUBLIC CALL BOX
NO!

VVVVWWWW
KRRZZAKK
SPAK
AOOW!
ALWAYS KEEP A GUN ON THE MAN WITH THE SONIC, HART.
"THERE WILL BE NO BATTLE HERE", AS A WISE MAN ONCE SAID.
IT WAS ME. I WAS THE WISE MAN.
YOU'RE A FOOL -- IT'LL KILL US ALL--
NO. IT WON'T. AND NEITHER WILL I, IF YOU DON'T BACK OFF AND LET THE GROWN-UPS TALK.
THINK ABOUT THAT, HART. THINK ABOUT THE VERY CLEAR PROMISE I AM MAKING.
I.
WILL NOT.
KILL YOU.
...MEN.
STAND DOWN.

LET HIM DEAL WITH IT.
I DON'T ENJOY SPEAKING YOUR LANGUAGE, HART.
BUT THAT'S WHAT THIS IS ALL ABOUT, ISN'T IT? EH? LANGUAGE. COMMUNICATION.
:: SIGNAL ::
EXACTLY!
AND IT'S NOT AN IT, HART. IT'S A HIM. OR A HER, PICK ONE.
BUT IT'S PEOPLE.
AUTONOMOUS REASONING CENTER! A WALKING, TALKING MIND THAT YOU'VE BEEN TORTURING FOR... HOW LONG, HART?
HOW MANY YEARS BEFORE IT FINALLY ESCAPED?
THAT'S -- THAT'S CLASSIFIED--
AND YOU KNEW. YOU KNEW ALL ALONG -- RUTHERFORD WAS JUST THE SCAPE-GOAT FOR THE COVER-UP--
DOCTOR, IT TRIED TO KILL JONES--
NOPE! HE HASN'T KILLED ANYONE. JUST NICE PEACEFUL COMAS.

:: ARC ::
SO WHAT WAS HE TRYING TO DO TO OUR FRIEND JONES, EH?
AUTONOMOUS MIND, FRESH OUT OF CAPTIVITY -- IT'S THE BIG QUESTION EVERYONE'S ASKING LATELY, WHAT DOES HE WANT?
REVENGE?
AH, BUT REVENGE IS BIG AND COMPLICATED AND VERY VERY HUMAN. ARC'S MOTIVES ARE ALIEN. AND SIMPLE.
HE'S A MIND.
HE WANTS TO KNOW THINGS.
HE WANTS TO LEARN.
TROUBLE IS, THERE'S ONLY SO MUCH YOU CAN LEARN FROM YOUR OWN PERSPECTIVE. IF YOU REALLY WANNA LEARN SOMETHING...
...YOU NEED TO LEARN FROM OTHER PEOPLE.
I GET IT.
HE'S NOT TRYING TO HURT PEOPLE. BUT ABSORBING THEIR INFORMATION -- TAKING IT OUT OF THEIR HEADS --
HE LIKES TO COME AND MEET US, BUT IT SORT OF...
...BLOWS OUR MINDS.

EXACTAMUNDO! BUT HE'S LEARNING ANOTHER WAY, AREN'T YOU, MISTER ARC?
:: THE SOUND ::
:: THE SOUND OF MY ::
:: VOICE ::
THE SOUND OF OUR VOICES. VERBAL COMMUNICATION.
NO NEED FOR INVASIVE OR VIOLENT METHODS OF INFORMATION RETRIEVAL, IT CAN BE A FREE EXCHANGE.
WE CAN JUST... TALK. AND UNDERSTAND. AND ONCE WE HAVE AN UNDERSTANDING...
WHEN YOU CAN UNDERSTAND... YOU DON'T HAVE TO DESTROY.
OOH, A-PLUS, DOCTOR RUTHERFORD.
HOPE FOR YOU YET.
NOW, I THINK ARC'S PROBLEM IS THAT HE'S BEEN ABSORBING INFORMATION ON THE FLY. WILLY-NILLY.
LET'S TRY SOMETHING MORE DIRECTED -- AN INTRODUCTORY PACKAGE, SO TO SPEAK.
LITTLE BASIC VOCAB. A GREETING. A GIFT.
HELLO, ARC.
I'M THE DOCTOR.

:: DOC ::
:: TORRRRR ::
:: HELLO, DOC-TORRR ::
:: ARC IS ::
:: PLEASED ::
:: TO MEET YOU ::
...
ALL RIGHT.
I'LL STAY.

WELL. ALL'S WELL THAT ENDS WELL, WHAT?
THE ARC'S RESTORED ALL THE VICTIMS, WITH NO HARM DONE. IF ANYTHING, I'M FEELING RATHER WELL-RESTED.
P. CARTWRIGHT DEPUTY ADMINISTRATOR

AND NOW THAT WE CAN COMMUNICATE WITH THE CREATURE'S MIND, WE'LL BE ABLE TO LEARN MUCH MORE ABOUT HOW ITS BODY WORKS...
SIR... WHERE IS IT NOW?
OH, THE MAN FROM THE MINISTRY SAID HE'D ESCORT IT BACK TO BALLARD'S LAB. LOVELY CHAP. GOT ON FAMOUSLY.

WHAT? THE DOCTOR'S NOT FROM THE MINISTRY! THE MAN'S A BLASTED SPY!
OH DEAR, ARE YOU SURE?
IF HE GETS THE CREATURE TO HIS SHIP--

VWOORRRP
VWOORRRP

OH DEAR.
WELL, NEVER MIND.
MY JOB'S SECURE.

PENNY FOR YOUR THOUGHTS?
HMM? OH, I WAS JUST THINKING ABOUT THE WEIRD ALIEN IN THE TARDIS.
THE WEIRD ALIEN WHO ESCAPED FROM HIS CAGE JUST TO SEE WHAT WAS OUT THERE.
AND HOW SOMETIMES IT HELPS TO SEE IT THROUGH SOMEONE ELSE'S EYES.
BUT THAT'S NOT SOMETHING YOU CAN DO WITH A STRAY, OR A PET, IS IT?
YOU NEED TO MAKE A FRIEND.
...WE'RE NOT TALKING ABOUT ARC, ARE WE?
CLEVER DOCTOR.
ALICE OBIEFUNE.
MAY I HAVE THE HONOR OF ESCORTING YOU TO YOUR MEETING WITH YOUR HORRIBLE LANDLORD?
...
YEAH, ACTUALLY -- YOU KNOW WHAT?
HE CAN WAIT.
LET'S GO SOMEWHERE FUN.
POLICE PUBLIC CALL BOX

COVER GALLERY

BBC NEW ADVENTURES WITH THE ELEVENTH DOCTOR
DOCTOR WHO
AL EWING
ROB WILLIAMS
SIMON FRASER
GARY CALDWELL

1B

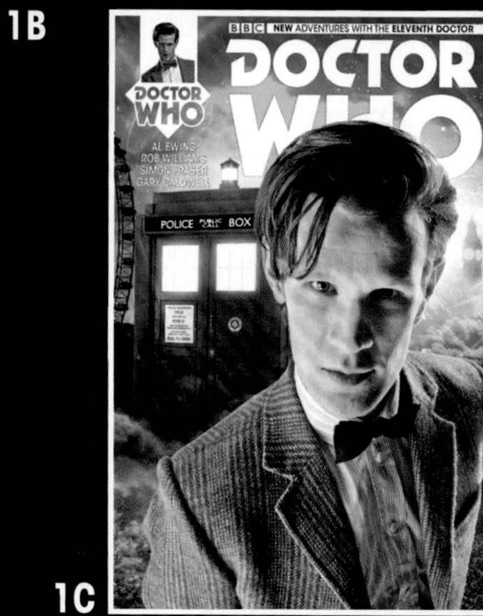

1C

2A

2B

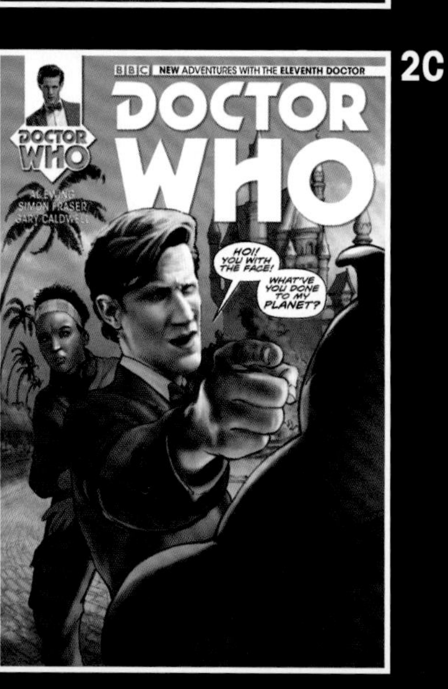

2C

3A

#1 B: Simon Fraser
#1 C: Rob Farmer
#2 A: Alice X. Zhang
#2 B: Rob Farmer
#3 A: Verity Glass

3B

3C

4A

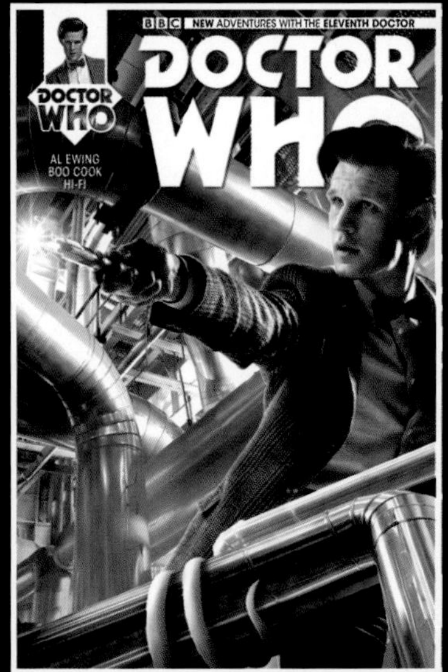

4B

5A

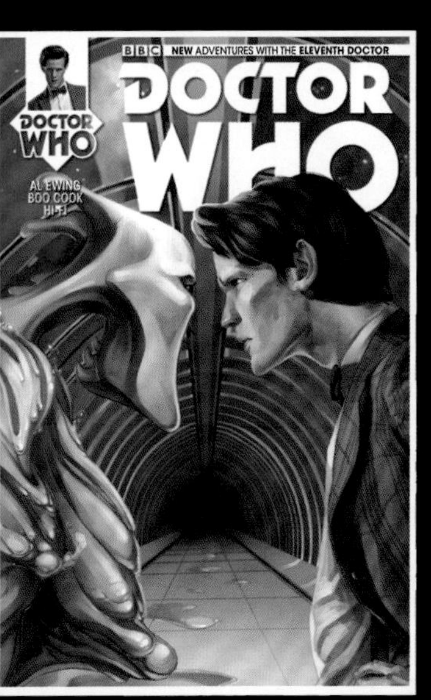

5B

#3 B: AJ
#3 C: Simon Fraser

#4 A: Verity Glass
#4 B: AJ

#5 A: Verity Glass
#5 B: AJ

DOCTOR WHO: THE TENTH DOCTOR VOL. 1: REVOLUTIONS OF TERROR

ISBN: 9781782761730

NICK ABADZIS
(EISNER AWARD-WINNER FOR *LAIKA*)

ELENA CASAGRANDE
(*SUICIDE RISK, ANGEL*)

COLLECTS DOCTOR WHO: THE TENTH DOCTOR ISSUES #1-5

ON SALE NOW - $19.99 / $22.95 CAN

AVAILABLE IN ALL GOOD COMIC STORES, BOOK STORES, AND DIGITAL PROVIDERS!

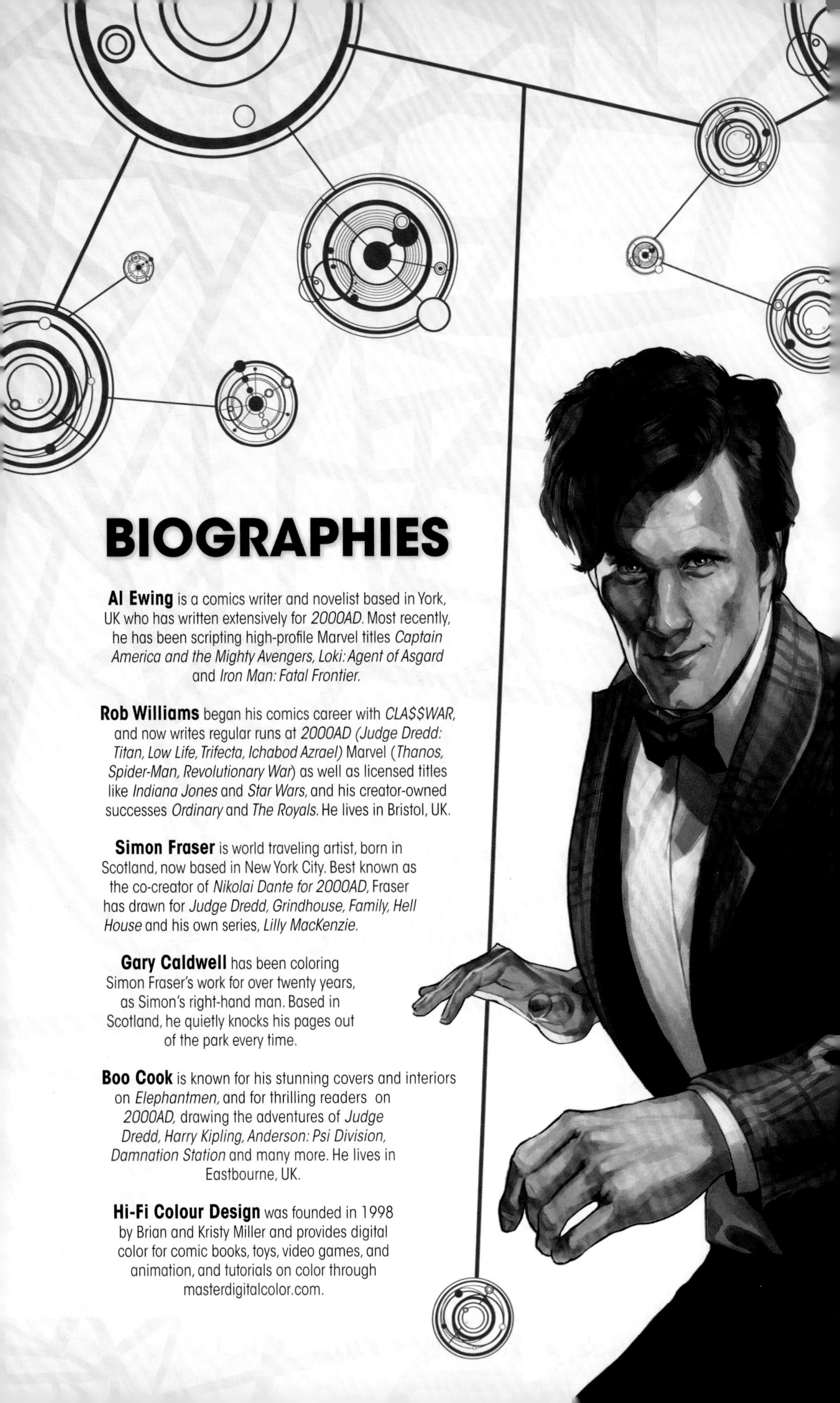

BIOGRAPHIES

Al Ewing is a comics writer and novelist based in York, UK who has written extensively for *2000AD*. Most recently, he has been scripting high-profile Marvel titles *Captain America and the Mighty Avengers, Loki: Agent of Asgard* and *Iron Man: Fatal Frontier.*

Rob Williams began his comics career with *CLA$$WAR*, and now writes regular runs at *2000AD (Judge Dredd: Titan, Low Life, Trifecta, Ichabod Azrael)* Marvel (*Thanos, Spider-Man, Revolutionary War*) as well as licensed titles like *Indiana Jones* and *Star Wars*, and his creator-owned successes *Ordinary* and *The Royals.* He lives in Bristol, UK.

Simon Fraser is world traveling artist, born in Scotland, now based in New York City. Best known as the co-creator of *Nikolai Dante for 2000AD*, Fraser has drawn for *Judge Dredd, Grindhouse, Family, Hell House* and his own series, *Lilly MacKenzie.*

Gary Caldwell has been coloring Simon Fraser's work for over twenty years, as Simon's right-hand man. Based in Scotland, he quietly knocks his pages out of the park every time.

Boo Cook is known for his stunning covers and interiors on *Elephantmen,* and for thrilling readers on *2000AD,* drawing the adventures of *Judge Dredd, Harry Kipling, Anderson: Psi Division, Damnation Station* and many more. He lives in Eastbourne, UK.

Hi-Fi Colour Design was founded in 1998 by Brian and Kristy Miller and provides digital color for comic books, toys, video games, and animation, and tutorials on color through masterdigitalcolor.com.